The Healthy Wok
CHINESE COOKBOOK

The Healthy Wok CHINESE COOKBOOK

Simple Recipes for Cooking
Healthy Versions of Your Favorite
Chinese Dishes at Home

CHARMAINE FERRARA

Foreword by Linda Ooi
Photography by Nadine Greeff

**ROCKRIDGE
PRESS**

Design by Rita Sowins
Photography © Nadine Greeff
Author photo © Janice Chong
Illustrations © Tom Bingham

ISBN: Print 978-1-62315-898-9 | eBook 978-1-62315-899-6

To Mum
for your persistent guidance
and unwavering support in the kitchen
and in life. I love you!

Contents

Foreword

THE LANGUAGE OF FOOD BRINGS PEOPLE AND CULTURES TOGETHER. In the food blogging world, our common interest in all things food-related often leads to encounters with other foodies from around the globe. Sometimes these interactions blossom into warm friendships, as was my experience with Charmaine Ferrara.

I first encountered Char's recipes and mouthwatering food photography on social media. Since we share a similar cultural background, I was curious about her blog *Wok & Skillet* and clicked to check out her recipes. As the author of two food blogs myself, I know how much work goes into creating a recipe and blog post. Char's dedication to detail and easy writing style make her recipes easy to follow and her blog posts a joy to read.

Like Char's blog, *The Healthy Wok Chinese Cookbook* is packed with goodies. If you're new to Chinese cooking, chapter 1 is a valuable primer, covering the essentials: ingredients, tools, utensils, techniques, and tips. The following eight chapters consist of 88 delicious family favorites and classic recipes that will deliver the delight of Chinese cuisine to your table.

Each recipe comes with helpful advice for substitutions, variations, and cooking and serving ideas. As most of us do not like to have to run to the store for just one or two missing ingredients, these suggestions offer the flexibility to experiment with the ingredients you have on hand and tailor the recipe to your own liking. The instructions are easy to follow and you should be able to create healthy and delicious Chinese meals for the family, or a superb dining experience for a crowd. I see this cookbook as a valuable resource, and your go-to for easy, healthy Chinese cuisine.

Char's culinary passion for cooking came from watching her grandma and mom cook in the kitchen at an early age. She began cooking for herself after she moved to the United States years later. In the process, she realized how much she really enjoys cooking and shares this experience with you through her blog and this book. In Char's words, "Cooking does not have to be intimidating . . . If I can do it, you can too."

—LINDA OOI, Author of RotiNRice.com and MalaysianChineseKitchen.com

Introduction

I GREW UP IN A TYPICAL MALAYSIAN CHINESE HOME—a full house with a very full dining table. My grandmother, or *ah mah* in Chinese (Hokkien dialect), walked to the market almost every morning to buy groceries, then spent most of her remaining day cooking a variety of delicious Chinese dishes for the whole family. I often lurked in the kitchen, watching her prepare the ingredients for each dish, then work her magic in the wok.

My first hands-on wok encounter occurred when I was about six years old. I had to use a stepstool so I could reach my ah mah's giant wok. My aunt, Bee Ee, hovered over me as I tossed rice into the wok. From the corner of my eye, I could see my ah mah shaking her head and giggling as I put ketchup and sugar in my fried rice (yeah, I know it sounds gross but I still remember that to my six-year-old sweet tooth, it was the best thing ever!). I now realize that the creative license I was given at that young age to add what I saw fit—even if nobody agreed with my choices—helped lay the foundation for my lifelong passion for food and cooking.

As I got to experience my mom's amazing cooking, this passion grew along with me. In addition to learning how to cook from my ah mah, my mom had also taken cooking classes with locally renowned chef and cooking instructor Dato' Lim Bian Yam. I was fortunate to grow up around very, *very* good food! Mostly I ate it; I didn't have a lot of experience cooking it.

When I first moved to the United States, I was struck by the differences between Chinese cuisine in the States and the traditional Chinese food I grew up with. The deep-fried every-thing covered in sugary neon-red sauces, and with hardly any vegetables, was definitely a culture shock for me.

Charmaine, 3, with her Ah Mah (grandmother) in Malaysia.

The author, 16, and her mother celebrate Ah Mah's (center) birthday.

I still remember my first Chinese meal in America—I ordered one of my favorite dishes, sweet and sour pork. What I thought would be lightly battered pieces of pork in a flavorful sweet and sour sauce turned out to be mostly oily batter pieces with very little meat, drenched in that sugary red sauce. The portion size was also a huge shock. I had enough on my plate for breakfast, lunch, *and* dinner! (Luckily, I would come to try many lovely Chinese dishes at fantastic Chinese restaurants in Eugene, Springfield, and Portland—though the portions were still much larger than I was used to.)

It was 2000, and I had moved to Oregon to attend university. Thousands of miles away from home and family, I had no choice but to learn how to cook for myself. I was determined to reproduce those Chinese dishes I missed so much. As I fumbled around in the kitchen, I tried my best to recall how my mom or ah mah would prepare the dish I was attempting to make. I suddenly realized, despite all those childhood moments spent in the kitchen, that I still had a lot to learn. This was my launching pad—I was forced to put my passion into action with a real working knowledge of how to cook the foods I loved!

I purchased my first wok and had no idea how to care for it. I panicked when I saw the wok covered in rust soon after I had washed it for the first time. I rushed to the Asian market thinking that the wok was ruined and that I'd need a new one. The store owner refused to sell me a new wok, and told me to go home, scrub out the rust on my wok, and season it. Lesson learned! I called my mom that evening and asked her how to properly season a wok.

My love for Chinese cooking and my cooking skills continued to grow, so much so that in 2012, I started my blog, *Wok & Skillet* (wokandskillet.com), to share my passion for simple and delicious recipes, and to demystify Chinese food.

In this book, I want to share how easy, fun, and flavorful healthy Chinese cooking can be. My time in the kitchen has taught me that being armed with a few key tools, techniques, and ingredients is all it takes to successfully make your favorite Chinese dishes at home.

The central tool? The wok. A wok is essential for authentic Chinese cooking and is the perfect medium for stir-frying, one of the healthiest cooking methods due to its traditional use of loads of vegetables and very little oil. The wok can transform humble ingredients into aromatic and flavor-packed meals in just minutes.

If you love Chinese food and want to master it, especially without consuming the extra calories that come with Chinese fast food, this book is for you. Here you'll find healthier versions of your Chinese restaurant favorites as well as some simple everyday dishes that you would see in a typical Chinese home kitchen.

You don't need a culinary degree to use a wok or to master Chinese cooking techniques. I am living proof of that. I'll walk you through every step. And the more you practice this wonderful cooking method, the easier it becomes. In doing so, you'll soon discover your own shortcuts, techniques, and flavor combinations that excite your palate—much like those I was invited to explore in my ah mah's kitchen.

I hope you see your favorite Chinese dishes in this book, along with some new ones that you will be inspired to try. Come join me, and together we will explore Chinese wok cooking that allows you to enjoy authentic favorites at home.

Welcome to the sizzling, steaming, stir-fry world of healthy Chinese wok cooking!

CHAPTER 1

Chinese Cooking at Home

A Healthier Alternative

Chinese takeout food has become synonymous with convenience in today's high-paced life. It may be quick and easy, and it may also taste great, but it is not always the healthiest option. In moving from the Far East to the Far West, I went from eating Chinese food virtually every day without thinking twice about nutrition, to limiting my American Chinese food intake for fear of gaining too much weight!

Some restaurants, though certainly not all, use low quality ingredients in order to keep their costs down. Consequently, they compensate by adding things like monosodium glutamate (MSG) and using more salt and sugar than necessary in order to make the food taste more appealing. Taste is king in restaurants, and so are portions that appear "good for the money."

BETTER THAN TAKEOUT

When you eat at a restaurant, it can be nearly impossible to tell just by looking at a dish what ingredients and additives were used to prepare it. By cooking at home, you have complete control over what goes, and what doesn't go, into your food. Below is a side-by-side comparison of the home-cooked and restaurant versions of a dish that has become a staple of American Chinese fast food:

GENERAL TSO'S CHICKEN	5.7-ounce serving of my recipe (page 85)	5.7-ounce serving at Panda Express
Calories	239	330
Calories from Fat	86	100
Total Fat	11g	12g
Saturated Fat	1g	2g
Sodium	690mg	910mg
Carbohydrates	6g	37g
Sugar	6g	15g
Protein	29g	19g

Cooking your own food at home always results in better quality and fresher, healthier dishes. You control every ingredient that goes into your dish, and no matter how heavy your hand, you will likely also use far less salt, fat, and oil than restaurants do.

You will quickly see how simple it is to make Chinese food at home. Like takeout, wok cooking is quite convenient, yet far healthier, and will also save you a lot of money in the long run—no tipping required!

Healthy Chinese Recipes

The recipes in this cookbook are not based on any specific diet, but they adhere to principles commonly found in any sensible healthy diet. This means no deep-fried foods, lower sodium and sugar, heart-healthy oils, creative seasoning, lean cuts of meat, and lots of colorful, fresh veggies.

Peanut oil is the best type of oil for Chinese cooking. It has a taste that complements most Chinese dishes and a high smoke point, making it perfect for stir-frying. High in unsaturated fats and low in saturated fats, peanut oil is very heart-healthy. If you or anyone in your family has a peanut allergy, olive oil is a good alternative.

When choosing meats, opt for leaner cuts whenever possible:

- **Chicken:** chicken breast over chicken thighs.
- **Pork:** pork shoulder or tenderloin over pork belly.
- **Beef:** cuts with less fat and marbling, such as top round or sirloin tip, over rib eye.

Eating healthy does not have to be complicated or restrictive. Even the simple step of cooking at home more, and dining out or ordering takeout less often, can be life-changing. And don't be afraid to splurge every once in a while.

Key Ingredients

Keep your pantry stocked with these essential ingredients so you can easily whip up healthy Chinese meals any time. You should be able to find these items at your local supermarket or Asian market. With the convenience of e-commerce, you can also have them delivered right to your doorstep.

Most Chinese dishes use the following ingredients as a base, so I always have them on hand. When I plan my meals for the week, I often just have to purchase meat (if I don't already have it in my freezer) and fresh vegetables.

BOTTLED SAUCES

SOY SAUCE: Most Asian dishes are not complete without at least a splash of soy sauce. Soy sauce is made from fermented soybeans and has a very deep, salty flavor. Soy sauce is used in many Asian cuisines in place of salt and as a condiment. It is sometimes also referred to as light soy sauce to differentiate it from dark soy sauce, which is much thicker. You can buy low-sodium soy sauces if you are watching your salt intake. Most soy sauces do contain wheat, so if you are on a gluten-free diet, use tamari instead.

DARK SOY SAUCE: This is used more for providing a rich, dark color to dishes than for flavor. Less salty than light soy sauce, it contains molasses, which also makes it sweeter. Light and dark soy sauces cannot be used in place of each other, but can amicably be used together. Dark soy sauce has a very intense dark color, so as you might expect, a little goes a long way.

SHAOXING WINE: This Chinese rice wine is commonly used in Chinese cooking for marinades and sauces. Made from fermented glutinous rice, it adds a nice flavor to dishes. Higher-quality Shaoxing wine can be enjoyed as a drink, but I would not recommend drinking the Shaoxing wines that you buy in the condiments aisle. Dry sherry can be used as a substitute for Shaoxing wine. Mirin is also a rice wine, but it should not be used as a substitute as it has a completely different flavor and is much sweeter.

OYSTER SAUCE: This sweet and salty sauce made from oyster extract and seasonings lends a rich, full-bodied flavor to any dish. Don't settle for cheap brands—they normally contain added MSG. Oyster sauce is naturally dark, but some brands add caramel for color and flavor. You can also find vegetarian oyster sauce made with mushrooms instead of oysters. Once opened, oyster sauce should be stored in the refrigerator.

SESAME OIL: Typically used in sauces and marinades, this aromatic oil is used for flavoring dishes rather than for frying. Because of its very strong fragrance, it can be used sparingly.

For Chinese cooking, dark toasted sesame oil is used, as opposed to the lighter sesame oil made from untoasted sesame seeds. Make sure you choose pure sesame oil and not a blend containing other types of oils.

HOISIN SAUCE: Made from fermented soybeans, garlic, five-spice powder, and other ingredients, hoisin sauce is sweet, pungent, and slightly salty. Often used as a barbecue sauce in Chinese cuisine, it is also famously served as a dipping sauce with Peking duck. It can also be used to flavor sauces. Hoisin sauce should be refrigerated after opening.

5 TIPS FOR KEEPING IT HEALTHY

Getting past unhealthy foods is a bit like getting over an old boyfriend. The more you know about the options and the more you experiment, the less likely it is that you will ever look back wistfully on those old, less healthy former favorites.

1. **Swap spices.** Increase flavor in a dish by adding spices and/or aromatics instead of sugar and salt. Fresh foods are naturally tasty and do not need much to boost their flavors, especially when cooked right.

2. **Maximize portion impact.** For a protein boost, add quinoa to your rice, and limit yourself to one small bowl per meal. Simply add one or two tablespoons of (rinsed) dried quinoa while the water is boiling and steam it together with the rice.

3. **Give veggies top billing.** Focus on vegetables as your main dish, shifting proteins and carbohydrates to the side. And your mom was right: for optimum health benefits, make it a habit to finish all the vegetables on your plate before adding more sides!

4. **Trick your tummy.** Use smaller plates and practice portion control. Studies have shown that smaller plates make the portion sizes look bigger, tricking our brains into thinking that we have eaten more than we really have.

5. **Map it out.** Plot out a good weekly meal-planning system to avoid last-minute takeout dinners. Many meal-planning systems exist, from printable spreadsheets to high-tech phone apps. Test a few and choose one that works for you.

DRY INGREDIENTS

WHITE PEPPER: In Chinese cooking, white pepper is used more often than black pepper. It is often sold as a fine powder, as opposed to more coarsely ground black pepper. Although it is spicy, it has a milder flavor than black pepper, and allows the flavors of the main ingredients in a dish to shine through.

CHICKEN STOCK GRANULES: Sometimes referred to as chicken bouillon powder, this "secret weapon" in Chinese kitchens is especially useful for adding a touch of flavor to cooked vegetables. It's essentially dehydrated chicken stock, but with additional seasonings. The flavor is less intense than bouillon cubes. I recommend buying products without added MSG (see Recommended Brands on page 166).

FIVE-SPICE POWDER: This highly aromatic mixture of finely ground cinnamon, star anise, fennel, cloves, and Sichuan peppercorns adds warm flavor and fragrance to a dish. A good five-spice blend should be very aromatic but not spicy. It is perfect as a dry rub, especially for barbecue, but can also be used in sauces. Very little is needed to convey loads of flavor.

DRIED SHIITAKE MUSHROOMS: Dried shiitake mushrooms add deep, savory flavor to Chinese dishes. Easily available at all Asian markets and some grocery stores, they can be stored in your pantry for months, if not years. Use whole mushrooms as the star ingredient in a dish, or slice them into thin strips to add depth of flavor. Simply soak them in a bowl of water overnight, or in a pinch, boil them for about 20 minutes to soften.

FRESH INGREDIENTS

GARLIC: In addition to being a flavoring agent, this ubiquitous bulb has been used in China for medicinal purposes for thousands of years. A key ingredient in any good stir-fry, minced garlic is used to flavor the cooking oil before other ingredients are added to the wok.

GINGER: Fresh ginger is another essential flavoring in Chinese cooking. It is often paired with garlic in stir-fries to flavor the cooking oil. Ginger has a spicy flavor when eaten raw, but when cooked, it imparts a gentler, unmistakable flavor and aroma to the dish. To peel ginger, simply scrape the skin off with the side of a metal spoon. From there it can be minced, very finely julienned, or sliced into thin pieces.

SCALLIONS: Also known as green onions or spring onions, scallions are used in almost any kind of Chinese dish. Raw scallions are often finely chopped to garnish dishes and soups. Larger pieces cooked very lightly can feature as an ingredient in a recipe. Their mild onion flavor does not overpower the flavor of a dish.

CLASSIC FLAVOR COMBINATIONS

Chinese flavor combinations abound and comprise any blend of salty, savory, sweet, sour, and sometimes bitter or spicy elements. Once you discover which flavors tantalize your palate, you're likely to seek out recipes that feature your favored combinations, and maybe eventually incorporate your favorites into dishes beyond Chinese cooking.

Fresh ingredients: Garlic, ginger, and scallions are sometimes referred to as the trinity of Chinese cooking. You will almost always find one of those three ingredients in a dish, and often all three.

Marinade: The purpose of the marinade in Chinese cooking is to season and tenderize meat and prepare it for stir-frying. Usually it's the salty and savory elements that are incorporated into the marinade (adding sugar at this stage causes meat to caramelize too quickly). Some combination of salt and/or soy sauce, white or black pepper, and cornstarch (for keeping the meat tender) is often all you will need.

Sauces: Sauce is often what makes a dish unique. This cookbook contains various sauce blends, including sweet, sour, salty, and spicy, as well as medleys comprised of several elements.

SHALLOTS: Shallots are a bit like red onion, but sweeter and milder in flavor, with a slight hint of garlic. They make a good substitute for onion. In Asia, crispy fried shallots are a popular condiment or garnish.

CILANTRO: Cilantro adds fresh, bright flavor to a dish. Because of its strong fragrance, it is seldom used as an actual ingredient, but commonly used as a garnish. Certain people with a specific gene (my husband being one of those people) experience a soapy aftertaste when eating cilantro. You may want to leave the cilantro on the side in case any of your family or guests have this genetic trait.

SEASONING YOUR WOK

Whether you choose a carbon steel wok or a cast iron wok, it's important to season the wok before you use it for the first time in order to prepare it for stir-frying and cooking. Seasoning a wok helps it create a natural patina, or a layer of nonstick coating, on the wok's surface.

As a bonus, this patina also subtly enhances the flavor of the foods that you cook in it. The more you cook with your wok, the more layers it builds up and the more patina it develops. Over time, this patina gives the wok a gorgeous dark color and a natural nonstick surface, along with imparting additional fantastic flavors to your meals.

How to Season a Wok

You will need the following:

- Brand-new cast iron or carbon steel wok
- Stainless steel scrubber
- Dish soap
- 2 tablespoons of peanut oil (or any other oil with a very high smoke point, like canola or grapeseed oil)
- 2-inch piece of ginger, peeled and sliced
- 1½ cups chopped scallions or garlic chives (cut into 2-inch pieces)

1. Carbon steel and cast iron woks are coated with a chemical to prevent them from rusting from the time they leave the factory until when they are purchased and used, so the first step is to remove the chemical. To do this, thoroughly scrub the wok, inside and out, with a stainless steel scrubber and a generous amount of dish soap in warm water.

2. After rinsing all the soap off, set the wok on a burner over medium heat. This will dry the wok and start to open up the pores of the metal (really!) to prep it for its very first seasoning.

3. As soon as the wok is completely dry and at the right temperature (water droplets flicked into the wok should sizzle immediately), add the peanut oil, ginger, and scallions to the wok.

4. Stir-fry for about 15 minutes, moving the vegetables all around the wok to completely cover the bottom and the sides of the wok.

5. Discard the ginger and scallions, and allow the wok to cool down slightly.

6. Using only water, rinse the wok, gently wiping off any food residue with a clean, damp sponge (without soap) or a bamboo wok brush.

7. Return the wok to the burner over medium heat to dry. Turn off the heat when the wok is completely dry.

8. You may need to repeat this seasoning process if you find that your wok imparts a "steely" taste to your food.

To maintain that lovely seasoning on your brand-new wok, hold off on cooking highly acidic foods like tomatoes, and avoid boiling water in the wok for poaching or steaming. Otherwise you may strip off that patina that you worked to develop! Allow the wok at least a few months of regular use before boiling water or cooking acidic foods in it.

Even if you use your wok frequently, it takes time to develop a nice patina, so don't feel discouraged if you don't see great results, even in the first year. As you use your new wok, feel free to reseason it as often as needed (steps 3 through 7 only), especially if you notice your wok is losing its nonstick capabilities—it just needs a little spa treatment!

Choosing a Wok

A wok is at the heart of every Chinese kitchen. This tool serves as the primary cookware for just about any cooking method, whether it is stir-frying, pan-frying, braising, boiling, deep-frying, or steaming. When it comes to choosing a wok, a good-quality wok is important, but more expensive does not always mean better. Let's explore.

If you are cooking for just one or two, a 12-inch wok will suffice. A 14-inch wok is an ample size for a family of four to six, and is the standard size used in most home kitchens. There are much larger woks—up to a few feet in diameter—but those are designed for restaurant use. I would not recommend a wok smaller than 12 inches, as it can be difficult to move food around in order to get a proper stir-fry. However, they do look pretty for presentation if you serve a dish in them.

I don't recommend nonstick woks for stir-frying because the high temperatures often required for stir-frying can cause the nonstick material to release toxic chemicals and even transfer some of the material to the food. Nonstick woks can still be used for making soups and steaming, but I would only recommend them for low-heat cooking.

CARBON STEEL WOK

A good carbon steel wok is the best option, and luckily, it is also the least expensive! Perfect for the home kitchen, carbon steel woks are light yet durable. As they are quite thin, they heat up very quickly and evenly.

Choose a carbon steel wok that is at least 14-gauge, as these are sturdy and won't bend. A carbon steel wok does need to be seasoned, and over time, this seasoning will help it develop a naturally nonstick surface. The more nonstick it becomes, the less oil you can use when cooking.

Most carbon steel woks have a wooden handle that stays cool as you cook. This is handy for when you want to flip your food in the wok without the wok spatula—a technique that will help you look like a real pro while you entertain your guests!

CAST IRON WOK

Traditional woks are made out of cast iron. They can be heavy and take time to heat up, but they retain heat well and cook food evenly. They also develop a nonstick surface readily after seasoning. Cast iron is a great option if your heat source is a gas burner, as it actually relies on very high heat to function at its best.

My mom has used cast iron woks for years. Because she uses it on a daily basis, it rests on her gas burner at all times. It is so well seasoned that it's easy to maintain. After cooking in the wok, she just gives it a good rinse, places it on the burner, turns on the heat to dry the wok, then turns off the heat once dry. There it will sit until the next time she uses it, which is usually the next meal!

On the down side, if you rarely cook with a wok (hopefully this cookbook will change that), it may be cumbersome to store such a bulky, heavy wok in a cupboard. It can also become difficult to maintain the seasoning.

Most cast iron woks have iron loop handles. Though these are helpful for picking up the heavy wok when it's cool, the handles get very hot when the wok is in use. Always use protective oven mitts or silicone holders when touching the handles or picking up the wok during or right after use.

FLAT-BOTTOM AND ROUND-BOTTOM WOKS

If you have a flat stove top (electric, glass-top, etc.), a flat-bottom wok works best, providing the most contact with the heat source.

On a gas range, a round-bottom wok is the better option. The flames from the gas stove can easily wrap around the curve of the wok, giving it more even heat distribution.

What if you already have a round-bottom wok but a flat stove top? You can use a wok ring to help keep the wok in place. Setting the wok ring upside down so the wok rests on the wider end of the ring can help distribute the heat more evenly. However, the heat distribution will still not be as good as when using a flat-bottom wok.

Care and Maintenance

Your wok can last for years and years if it is properly cared for. But even though you want it to develop that great patina and seasoning, it still needs to be cleaned after each use. Below are some tips for cleaning your wok without losing that nice coating:

HOW TO CLEAN A WOK

1. Rinse the wok while gently scraping any food residue off the surface with a wok brush or soapless stainless steel scrubber. If you have any stubborn bits stuck to your wok, place the wok on a burner over medium heat and add a splash of water to help loosen those bits.

2. Once rinsed and scraped, heat the wok over medium heat to thoroughly dry it. When it's completely dry, turn off the heat.

3. Pour about a tablespoon of peanut oil into the wok. Use a folded paper towel to spread the oil all over the wok's inside surface. (For very well-seasoned woks, you can skip this step, as there should now be enough of a patina to keep it oiled and rust-free.)

While soap should be avoided as much as possible, especially for new woks, it is okay to use a very little bit of soap on a seasoned wok from time to time. I use a touch of soap whenever I cook anything spicy, just to wash off those chili oils on the surface, so my next dish won't pick up any of that flavor.

Because, like my mom, I use my wok daily, it stays on my stove top. If you don't use your wok as often, store it with the wok lid on so it won't collect dust.

Tools and Utensils

Most Chinese dishes can be prepared using the pots and pans you already have in your kitchen, but you can invest in some basic equipment and tools to enhance your Chinese cooking experience. As already mentioned, a wok is the one absolute must-have. In addition, here are some tools that you would see in a typical Chinese kitchen. Please don't feel like you need to go on a shopping spree to buy these; you may never need certain items—I simply find these most useful for my needs. Start with a wok (with a wok ring if you need it), and a wok spatula, then slowly build your collection as you expand your Chinese cooking repertoire.

BAMBOO STEAMER: Small bamboo steamers are famously used for dim sum, but various sizes can be used to steam meats, fish, vegetables, and buns. You'll need a bamboo steamer that will sit high enough in your wok so water can boil under it; a steamer of about 10 inches or larger is a safe bet. To steam, simply add water to your wok (about halfway to the bottom of your steamer), allow the water to boil, then set your steamer in the wok above the water.

CHEF'S KNIFE OR CLEAVER: A good sharp knife is an essential tool for any kitchen, Chinese or not. The cleaver is a common knife in the Chinese kitchen due to its versatility. There are small cleavers delicate enough to chop vegetables, and there are heavy cleavers sharp enough to cut pork ribs into little pieces. A good chef's knife is perfectly adequate for Chinese cooking if you find a cleaver intimidating.

METAL STEAMING RACK: This round rack can be used to steam larger dishes that won't fit in a bamboo steamer. It rests in the wok, allowing you to place heatproof dishes right in the wok. This rack is perfect for reheating fried rice, steaming whole fish, and making dishes like Steamed Egg with Ground Pork (page 96).

RICE COOKER: You can cook rice on the stove top (see pages 20 and 22), but if you're cooking a lot of Asian food, a rice cooker is an incredibly convenient kitchen appliance to have. Just put the rinsed rice in the rice cooker, fill it with water to the level marked, and turn it on. You'll never undercook or burn rice again! You can also cook brown rice and quinoa in a rice cooker. Most modern rice cookers also come with a steamer basket so you can steam food while you cook your rice.

SKIMMER: Also known as a spider, this tool is perfect for blanching vegetables, straining noodles, and deep-frying. A skimmer allows you to easily scoop any food from the water or oil in your wok. Larger skimmers are great for noodles and vegetables, and smaller skimmers are ideal for deep-frying.

WOK BRUSH: Made with thin strips of bamboo, a wok brush is used to clean the wok. The bamboo easily removes food residue that is stuck on the wok's surface—just add water to the hot wok, then brush the tool in a swirling motion to clean it. A stainless steel scrubber (without soap) will also work in place of a wok brush.

WOK LADLE: Built with a different angle than a traditional ladle, a wok ladle is useful for stirring soups in a wok and transferring soup to serving bowls. Many Chinese chefs also use this ladle to scoop sauces into their stir-fries. It is usually a deep, round metal bowl on a long metal body, with a wooden handle at the end.

WOK LID: A wok lid is essential for steaming dishes when using a metal steaming rack, and also for braising meats. Wok lids are normally made of aluminum and are quite light. I recommend using the lid when storing your wok to protect it from dust.

WOK RING: You may or may not need this, depending on what type of wok you use and what type of stove top you have. The primary function of a wok ring is to keep a round-bottom wok in position when using it on a flat stove top.

WOK SPATULA: A wok spatula goes hand in hand with a wok. In my experience, you just can't have one without the other. I discourage using any other type of spatula with a wok, and here's why: A wok spatula is designed with a rounded edge that should fit the curve of the wok, making it very easy to scrape food from the wok, collecting it all and leaving hardly any residue. It's the perfect utensil for stir-frying.

Basic Cooking Techniques

Now that you have your wok equipment and your pantry is stocked, let's check out a handful of basic cooking techniques so you can make Chinese food at home sucessfully.

Before any cooking begins, the first thing a wise cook will do is read the recipe thoroughly. Don't just read the ingredients to make a shopping list; look over the recipe with a critical eye. Pay attention to how each ingredient is prepared for that dish, walking through each step in your mind's eye. This will help you prepare as you consider all the items, time, and space you will need—allowing you to breeze through your recipe like the host of a cooking show!

CUTTING

While it is visually important that ingredients are cut with care so they look pretty in a dish, your taste buds expect that the ingredients will have cooked evenly. For example, if you have julienned carrots in a stir-fry, your taste buds would be disappointed to discover that some carrot pieces were overcooked and soggy because they were so thin, while other carrot pieces were undercooked because they were too large. In order to please all the senses, here are some cutting techniques you'll be encouraged to employ in this book:

DICE: Cut into long strips, turn the strips horizontally, and cut the strips into cubes.

CHOP: Place the ingredient horizontally on the cutting board. While keeping the tip of the knife on the cutting board, push the blade down and slightly forward at the same time. Use your non-knife hand to slowly push the food toward the knife, keeping your knuckles and fingers out of harm's way.

JULIENNE: Cut into thin strips, stack a few strips at a time, and slice finely to make very thin matchstick-size pieces. When julienning ginger, cut into super-fine pieces.

MINCE: Cut into thin strips first then dice the strips. Hold the tip of the knife down with your free hand and gently chop, moving from side to side until all the pieces are evenly minced.

SLICE: If needed, cut the food (usually a large vegetable) in half or cut a thin section off the bottom so it will sit flat and stable on the work surface. Cut into even ¼ inch thick slices (thickness may vary depending on the ingredient and the recipe).

COOKING

Before the introduction of modern cookware and kitchen appliances, the wok was used in Chinese cuisine for literally all cooking methods, including roasting and smoking. Today, the most common cooking techniques using a wok are parboiling and blanching, steaming, and, of course, stir-frying.

PARBOILING AND BLANCHING: In some recipes, denser vegetables and meats are boiled for a short time to partially cook them, followed by stir-frying, grilling, or braising, which completes the cooking process. This parboiling process speeds up the cooking time and also helps foods cook more evenly. Blanching involves a bit of parboiling followed by "shocking" them (submerging them in cold water immediately after they are taken out of the hot water) in order to quickly stop the cooking process. For vegetables, blanching also helps set their bright green color.

STEAMING: Steaming is one of the healthiest cooking methods because it retains the nutrients in the ingredients and does not require oil. You can use a bamboo steamer or place your ingredients in a heatproof dish on a metal steaming rack. The design of the lid of a bamboo steamer handily allows some steam to escape instead of allowing water condensation to fall onto the food. A bamboo steamer is ideal for dim sum dishes and buns and protects them from sogginess. Using a metal steaming rack is convenient for larger food like fish and vegetables, and even for steaming leftover rice, which can benefit from a few droplets of condensation.

STIR-FRYING: Not only is stir-frying quick and healthy, it is also fun to do and results in delicious dishes. Bite-size pieces of food are tossed in a wok over high heat to seal in the flavor. Very little oil is used if the wok is well seasoned. Stir-frying is incredibly versatile since you can use just about any combination of vegetables and meats that you have on hand. When stir-frying vegetables, keep them constantly moving in the wok. For meats, you can leave them for a bit more time before moving them around in the wok, to allow them to sear.

One important component of any successful stir-fry is learning to control the heat of the wok. This will take some practice and familiarity with your burner or stove, as well as your wok. High heat is generally required for a good stir-fry, but heat that's too high for too long can result in burnt food. Medium-high heat is a safe place to be, but if the food starts browning too fast, don't be afraid to turn it down and fine-tune the heat as you cook.

- **Dry Stir-Fry:** Dry stir-frying is a method popular in Sichuan cuisine. Very little oil is used, and the meat or vegetable is dry-fried without any coating or batter. The cooking time is slightly longer but it produces a unique crispy, charred texture. A small amount of strong aromatics and very little sauce are added after the meat or vegetable is dry-fried.
- **Moist Stir-Fry:** In a moist stir-fry, stock or water is added to the dish while cooking to create an accompanying sauce or gravy. This is common in American-Chinese cuisine, as evidenced by dishes like Moo Goo Gai Pan (page 87) and Happy Family (page 68). Rice is often served with moist stir-fry dishes to help absorb the flavorful sauce.
- **Velvet Stir-Fry:** Velveting is a technique in which meats are marinated in liquids such as soy sauce, egg white, or Shaoxing wine, along with cornstarch. This starchy blend tenderizes the meat by acting as a protective barrier when stir-frying over high heat, locking in all the juices. The meat is sometimes blanched in hot oil or boiling water before stir-frying. This method results in super-soft and tender meat.

6 EASY STEPS TO STIR-FRYING

Because stir-frying is so healthy, easy, and delicious, it's a great technique to master and to make a regular part of your cooking routine. Most of your time will be spent preparing the ingredients. In fact, the stir-frying process literally takes just minutes, so you'll want to be ready with all your prepped ingredients before you fire up the wok. Follow these easy steps for a successful stir-fry every time:

1. **Prepare the ingredients.** This includes cutting any meat into thin strips or slices, chopping vegetables, and mixing the sauce. Mixing the sauce ahead of time is essential; you won't have the time to measure each sauce ingredient once the meat and vegetables are in the wok, since your hands will be busy stirring!

2. **Heat the wok.** Unless specified in the recipe, wait until the wok is sizzling hot before adding any oil. When water droplets sprinkled on the wok's surface sizzle immediately, it's ready. Use an oil with a high smoke point such as peanut oil or grapeseed oil.

3. **Sear meat first.** Using a wok spatula, arrange the meat strips in a single layer. Allow the bottom side of the meat to sear before flipping and moving the pieces around the wok. Remove the meat from the wok once cooked (unless directed otherwise).

4. **Add the vegetables.** If the wok is dry after removing the meat, add a splash of oil. Add aromatics such as garlic and/or ginger to

flavor the oil then add the vegetables in the order of their cooking time (slowest to fastest). Unless they are parboiled, firmer vegetables like broccoli and carrot slices take longer to cook than softer vegetables like leafy greens, fresh mushrooms, and fresh bean sprouts.

5. **Sauce and toss.** Add the sauce, stirring to combine all the ingredients. If there is cornstarch in the sauce, it will thicken very quickly. Thinner sauces should not sit in the wok for more than about 30 seconds, as they will burn quickly and overcook the food. Generally, once I add the sauce, I give it a quick stir to combine then remove the contents from the wok within about 10 seconds.

6. **Serve it.** Transfer the dish to a serving plate, add the garnish, and serve immediately. Enjoy!

Basic Sambal (Red Chili Sauce), page 29

The Basics

STEAMED WHITE RICE

2 cups jasmine rice
3 cups water, plus water
for rinsing the rice

SERVES 4 TO 6 AS PART OF A MULTICOURSE MEAL /
PREP TIME: 5 MINUTES / COOK TIME: 25 MINUTES

As sure as there are chopsticks on the Chinese table, there is rice. In a typical Chinese household, you'll find a variety of dishes in the middle of the dining table for all to share, and one bowl or plate of rice per person. That is what we call "family style" dining, and we do a lot of it.

1. First wash the rice. Pour the rice into a medium pot. Rinse the rice by filling the pot halfway with cold tap water, running your fingers through the rice to loosen the starch, then pouring out the murky water. Repeat three or four times, draining as much water as possible. Alternatively, put the rice in a mesh strainer and rinse it under running tap water.

2. To cook the rice, pour 3 cups of water over the rice in the pot.

3. Bring to a boil over high heat, uncovered.

4. When most of the water has been absorbed and you can see the surface of the rice, reduce the heat to low and cover the pot with a lid. (If you use a pot with a heavy base that retains heat well, you can turn off the heat completely at this point, leaving it covered. The rice will continue to steam and won't burn.)

5. Simmer the rice for an additional 12 minutes. No peeking!

6. Turn off the heat. Allow the rice to sit, covered, for 5 minutes.

7. Uncover. Just before serving, fluff the rice using a spatula or chopsticks.

Cooking Tip

In step 4, if the white foamy water starts to boil over once the pot is covered, remove the lid and allow more water to evaporate before covering the pot again.

Healthy Cooking Tip

To sneak in some protein, add 1 to 2 tablespoons of rinsed quinoa while the water is boiling.

STEAMED BROWN RICE

2 cups medium- or long-grain
  brown rice
4 cups water, plus more
  for rinsing the rice
1 teaspoon salt

SERVES 4 TO 6 AS PART OF A MULTICOURSE MEAL /
PREP TIME: 5 MINUTES / COOK TIME: 45 MINUTES

I find it encouraging that Chinese restaurants are serving brown rice as an alternative to white rice. Brown rice is high in fiber and essential minerals.

1. First wash the rice. Pour the rice into a medium pot. Rinse the rice by filling the pot halfway with cold tap water, running your fingers through the rice to loosen the starch, then pouring out the murky water. Repeat three or four times, draining as much water as possible. Alternatively, put the rice in a mesh strainer and rinse it under running tap water.

2. To cook the rice, pour 4 cups of water into the pot with the rice, then add the salt. Bring to a boil over high heat, uncovered.

3. When most of the water has been absorbed and the top of the rice is visible, reduce the heat to low and cover the pot.

4. Simmer the rice for 20 minutes. No peeking!

5. Turn off the heat. Let the rice sit, partially uncovered, for 15 minutes.

6. Fluff with a spatula or chopsticks before serving.

STEAMED QUINOA

2 cups quinoa
2½ cups water

SERVES 4 TO 6 AS PART OF A MULTICOURSE MEAL /
PREP TIME: 5 MINUTES / COOK TIME: 20 MINUTES

Since most Chinese dishes are paired with rice, steamed quinoa is a fantastic option for those of us who are watching our carb intake. Quinoa is actually a seed, not a grain. It is a complete protein, containing all the essential amino acids we need in our diet. Quinoa can also be cooked in a rice cooker.

1. Put the quinoa in a fine mesh strainer and rinse well under running tap water.

2. Pour the rinsed quinoa into a medium pot, and add the water.

3. Over medium-high heat, bring the water to a boil, uncovered.

4. When the water starts to boil, reduce the heat to low, cover the pot, and cook for 15 minutes.

5. Turn off the heat and uncover the pot. Fluff the quinoa with a fork then let it sit for about 5 minutes before serving.

Cooking Tip

To boost the flavor, cook quinoa in chicken stock instead of water (or use a combination of both).

CONGEE

1 cup short-grain rice
2-inch piece ginger, peeled
6 cups water

SERVES 4 TO 6 AS PART OF A MULTICOURSE MEAL /
PREP TIME: 5 MINUTES / COOK TIME: 1 HOUR

Congee is a rice porridge that is a mainstay at breakfast or brunch in China. It is Chinese comfort food at its best, and often the first dish I think of when I am ill. It can be served with a variety of toppings, so congee never gets boring! For really silky, thick congee, use short-grain or sushi rice. If it gets too thick, simply add more water to thin it to your preferred consistency.

1. First wash the rice. Pour the rice into a medium pot. Rinse the rice by filling the pot halfway with cold tap water, running your fingers through the rice to loosen the starch, then pouring out the murky water. Repeat three or four times, draining as much water as possible. Alternatively, put the rice in a mesh strainer and rinse it under running tap water.

2. Put the rice, ginger, and 6 cups of water in a medium pot.

3. Bring to a boil over high heat, reduce the heat to low and simmer, partially uncovered, for about 1 hour, stirring occasionally.

4. Serve with your favorite congee toppings (see Serving Tip).

Serving Tip

Serve with chopped scallions and/or cilantro, garlic oil, soy sauce, shredded chicken, sautéed spinach, hard-boiled egg, 1,000-year-old egg, hard-boiled salted egg, julienned ginger, fried fish . . . the list goes on.

BASIC CHINESE CHICKEN STOCK

1 whole chicken
2 large carrots, peeled
   and quartered
1 large yellow onion, peeled
   and halved
3 scallions
2-inch piece ginger, peeled
10 to 15 cups water

MAKES 8 TO 13 CUPS / PREP TIME: 5 MINUTES /
COOK TIME: 3 TO 4 HOURS

Good chicken stock is the foundation of great soups, but it can add so much flavor to other dishes as well. Chinese chicken stock uses slightly different ingredients than Western-style chicken stock, so try this version with the recipes in this book.

1. Put the chicken, carrots, onion, scallions, and ginger in a very large pot.

2. Fill the pot with just enough water to cover the chicken.

3. Simmer on low heat for 3 to 4 hours, partially uncovered. Use an ultra-fine mesh skimmer to remove any froth from the surface, along with any excess oil.

4. Allow the stock to cool slightly then remove the solid ingredients.

5. Run the stock through a fine mesh strainer as you pour it into storage jars or containers. You can refrigerate the stock overnight then simply scoop off the solidified fat. The stock will keep in the refrigerator for up to 1 week and in the freezer for up to 6 months.

Storage Tip

Disposable breast milk storage bags are the perfect solution for freezing chicken stock as they are easy to fill, seal well, and don't take up much space in the freezer.

ALL-PURPOSE STIR-FRY SAUCE

¼ cup low-sodium soy sauce

¼ cup oyster sauce

2 tablespoons Shaoxing wine

2 tablespoons honey
    or brown sugar

2 tablespoons water

1½ tablespoons sesame oil

1 tablespoon cornstarch

1 teaspoon chicken stock
    granules (see page 6)

Pinch ground white pepper

MAKES ABOUT 1 CUP / PREP TIME: 5 MINUTES

This stir-fry sauce takes only a few minutes to put together and goes with just about anything, including (but not only) Mixed Vegetable Stir-Fry (page 59). So instead of scrambling around your kitchen looking for various sauces to toss into your wok, keep this in a jar in the refrigerator.

1. Pour all the ingredients into a small jar or sealable container.

2. Shake until well combined.

3. Store in the refrigerator for up to 2 weeks.

Ingredient Tip

If you prefer a thinner, lighter sauce, skip the cornstarch.

SWEET AND SOUR SAUCE

5 tablespoons ketchup

3 tablespoons water

1½ tablespoons apple
cider vinegar

1 tablespoon plum sauce

1 tablespoon cornstarch

2 teaspoons soy sauce

2 teaspoons brown sugar

MAKES 1 CUP / PREP TIME: 5 MINUTES

I am pretty certain you'll agree that this recipe beats that neon-red sweet and sour sauce that comes in little packets with your Chinese takeout. This sauce can be included in a stir-fry or used as a dipping sauce. If using it for stir-fry, it must be cooked (recipes indicate when to add it). See the cooking tip for dipping sauce directions. Give it a try!

1. Combine all the ingredients in a small bowl.

2. Stir well to combine, using the back of the spoon to break up any cornstarch clumps, until the cornstarch has completely dissolved.

Cooking Tip

For a dipping sauce, you can either prepare this without the cornstarch and water, and serve it immediately (cold), or add the cornstarch and water, and heat it on the stove top until it thickens, to be served warm. Enjoy this dipping sauce with spring rolls, wontons, or even shrimp cocktail.

BROWN SAUCE

1 cup Basic Chinese Chicken
    Stock (page 25), or
    store bought
2 tablespoons oyster sauce
1 tablespoon soy sauce
2 teaspoons cornstarch
1 teaspoon brown sugar
½ teaspoon sesame oil

MAKES 1 CUP / PREP TIME: 5 MINUTES

Much like the All-Purpose Stir-Fry Sauce (page 26), this sauce is also exceedingly versatile. However, it carries a slightly different flavor and the texture is more thick and velvety. To use this sauce, cook the proteins and vegetables in the wok first, then add the sauce to the wok at the last minute.

1. Put all the ingredients in a small bowl and stir to combine. Stir well before using.

2. Alternatively, put all the ingredients in a small jar, seal, and gently shake to combine. Shake well before using.

Serving Tip

Brown sauce is great with noodles as well as rice. It also pairs very nicely with seafood, especially shrimp and scallops.

BASIC SAMBAL (RED CHILI SAUCE)

6 fresh red chiles
2 garlic cloves, chopped
1 small shallot, thinly sliced
1 teaspoon freshly squeezed
   lime juice
Pinch salt

MAKES ABOUT ¾ CUP / PREP TIME: 5 MINUTES

Sambal adds a spicy kick to just about any dish. It can be used as a condiment or as an ingredient in a dish like Spicy Sambal Fried Rice (page 152). If you're daring, add a Thai bird's eye chile for extra heat.

1. Remove the seeds from the chiles, then cut the chiles into thin slices.

2. Put the sliced chiles, garlic, and shallot into a small blender or food processor. Blend for a few seconds or until it forms a paste. Alternatively, use a mortar and pestle to mash the ingredients.

3. Once the mixture is a paste, add the lime juice and salt. Stir to combine.

Substitution Tip

I recommend using calamansi limes, which have a slightly orangey flavor. If you are unable to find them, regular limes will do just fine. You can also replace the lime with rice vinegar to give it a stronger vinegar essence.

Chinese Chicken Salad Cups, page 40

Appetizers & Dim Sum

SHRIMP DUMPLINGS

1 pound peeled and deveined
shrimp, roughly chopped
¼ cup diced water chestnuts
1½ tablespoons sesame oil
2 teaspoons soy sauce
2 tablespoons cornstarch
2 tablespoons finely chopped
fresh cilantro (optional)

FOR THE WRAPPERS

1¼ cups wheat starch
2 tablespoons tapioca flour
1¼ cups boiling water
1 teaspoon peanut oil

MAKES 15 TO 20 DUMPLINGS / PREP TIME: 45 MINUTES /
COOK TIME: 5 MINUTES

Shrimp dumplings, or *har gao*, is one of the most popular
dim sum dishes after *shumai*. Picture flavorful shrimp
and crunchy water chestnuts wrapped in soft and delicate
dumpling dough—they're irresistible! The wheat starch
in the dough gives the dumplings an almost translucent
appearance. It may take a bit of practice to get the wrapper
right, but it is well worth the effort.

TO MAKE THE FILLING

1. In a large bowl, combine the shrimp, water chestnuts,
sesame oil, soy sauce, and cornstarch. Add the cilantro
(if using). Mix well.

2. Marinate the mixture in the refrigerator for at least
30 minutes.

TO MAKE THE WRAPPERS

1. In a large bowl, combine the wheat starch and
tapioca flour.

2. Slowly pour the boiling water into the flour mixture while
stirring, until it starts to form a ball of dough.

3. Cover the bowl with a damp towel and allow the dough
to cool down slightly before handling.

4. Cover your palms, a small rolling pin, and a cutting board
with a bit of peanut oil to prevent the dough from sticking.

5. Knead the dough for 2 to 3 minutes.

6. Take about a teaspoon of dough and gently roll it
into a ball.

7. Roll the dough out into a small pancake, about 3 inches
in diameter.

Place about 1 teaspoon of shrimp filling in the middle of the dumpling wrapper.

On one side of the wrapper, pinch the edge continuously to make pleats.

Fold the other side of the wrapper toward the pleated side.

Gently press the edges together to seal the dumpling.

1. Set up a bamboo steamer in a wok. Line the steamer with parchment paper liners or napa cabbage leaves.

2. Place about 1 teaspoon of shrimp filling in the middle of a wrapper.

3. Make pleats on one side of the wrapper, then fold the other side of the wrapper toward the pleated side to seal the dumpling.

4. Repeat with the remaining filling and wrappers.

5. Place the dumplings in the bamboo steamer and steam for about 5 minutes or until cooked through.

Substitution Tip

If you can't find tapioca flour, you can use cornstarch. I find the texture a bit more grainy, but it works. You can also find dumpling flour at most Asian markets. Just add hot water and knead!

Better Than Takeout

A single dumpling in this recipe has 84 milligrams of sodium. Compare that to the 200 milligrams in a single shrimp dumpling from P.F. Chang's!

STEAMED VEGETABLE DUMPLINGS

FOR THE DUMPLINGS

2 teaspoons olive oil

4 cups shredded cabbage

1 carrot, shredded

2 scallions, chopped

5 to 8 garlic chives, cut into
 1-inch pieces

1-inch piece of ginger,
 peeled and minced

1 tablespoon water

2 teaspoons sesame oil, plus
 2 teaspoons for brushing

Salt

Pepper

15 to 20 round wonton
 wrappers

FOR THE DIPPING SAUCE

2 tablespoons soy sauce

2 teaspoons sesame oil

2 teaspoons rice vinegar

1 teaspoon chili oil

1-inch piece of ginger, peeled
 and finely minced

MAKES 15 TO 20 DUMPLINGS / PREP TIME: 20 MINUTES /
COOK TIME: 10 MINUTES

These vegetarian-friendly dumplings are the perfect appetizer that everybody will love—including those of us who are
so used to meat-filled dumplings. These dumplings prove
that vegetables are far from boring; they are incredibly
flavorful and versatile.

1. In a wok over medium heat, heat the olive oil.

2. Add the cabbage, carrot, scallions, garlic chives, and
ginger to the wok. Stir-fry for about 1 minute.

3. Add the water to help steam the vegetables. Stir-fry
until most of the water has evaporated. Drizzle 2 teaspoons
of sesame oil over the vegetables. Season with salt and
pepper, and toss. Remove from the heat and set it aside
to cool.

4. Place about 1 teaspoon of vegetable mixture in the middle of a wonton wrapper.

5. Dampen the edges of the wonton wrapper with a little
water, fold the wrapper in half so that it forms a triangle,
and gently press down to seal the edges.

6. Brush the dumplings with a light coating of sesame oil.

7. Line a bamboo steamer with parchment paper liners or napa cabbage leaves. Arrange the dumplings on top and steam for 8 minutes, or until the wonton wrappers look slightly translucent.

8. While the dumplings are steaming, make the dipping sauce. Combine the soy sauce, sesame oil, rice vinegar, chili oil, and ginger in a small bowl.

9. Serve the dumplings with the dipping sauce.

Variation Tip

Add your favorite veggies to make this dish your own. Some great options are bell pepper, shiitake mushrooms, and spinach. Shred them finely so they fit easily into the dumpling. Some diced water chestnuts or green peas add a nice crunch, if desired.

PORK AND SHRIMP SHUMAI

½ pound shrimp, peeled
  and deveined
½ pound ground pork
3 tablespoons sesame oil
1 tablespoon cornstarch
1 tablespoon soy sauce
1 teaspoon grated ginger
½ teaspoon salt
2 pinches ground white pepper
2 teaspoons Shaoxing wine
20 to 25 round wonton
  wrappers
½ carrot, finely minced

MAKES 20 TO 25 SHUMAI / PREP TIME: 20 MINUTES /
COOK TIME: 10 MINUTES

There are quite a few versions of shumai, but this is a dim sum classic. The pork and shrimp combination gives the shumai incredible flavor and texture. Steaming helps keep the shumai super moist. The best part is, they are incredibly easy to make!

1. Mince the shrimp by flattening each piece with the side of a knife, then roughly chopping each one.

2. Mix together the shrimp and the ground pork.

3. Add the sesame oil, cornstarch, soy sauce, ginger, salt, pepper, and Shaoxing wine to the shrimp and pork. Combine thoroughly.

4. Make an "O" with your thumb and index finger. Place one wonton wrapper on the "O" and gently press it down to create a small cup.

5. Using a teaspoon, fill the wonton cup to the top with some of the pork and shrimp mixture. Use the back of the teaspoon to press the filling into the cup.

6. Line a bamboo steamer with parchment paper liners or napa cabbage leaves. Arrange the shumai on top of the liners or leaves. Top each shumai with a bit of minced carrot.

7. Steam for 10 minutes or until the meat is cooked through.

Cooking Tip

You can steam a large batch and freeze some. Whenever you are in the mood for shumai, simply place a few frozen shumai in a bamboo steamer and steam for about 8 minutes.

COLD SESAME NOODLES

6 ounces whole-grain spaghetti

2 tablespoons sesame
oil, divided

2 tablespoons soy sauce

1 tablespoon rice vinegar

2 teaspoons brown sugar
or honey

2 teaspoons peanut butter

1 carrot, julienned

1-inch piece ginger, peeled
and minced

2 scallions, chopped

1 tablespoon sesame seeds

SERVES 6 TO 8 AS PART OF A MULTICOURSE MEAL /
PREP TIME: 10 MINUTES / COOK TIME: 15 MINUTES

These refreshing noodles are a perfect summertime treat that
you don't have to feel guilty about indulging in. The recipe
gives you healthy whole-grain noodles coated in a tantalizing
sauce, topped with crunchy carrots, ginger, scallions, and
sesame seeds. It's meant to be an appetizer, but nobody will
mind if this ends up becoming a full meal.

1. Cook the spaghetti according to the package directions
for al dente. Rinse the noodles under cold water and toss
in 1 tablespoon of sesame oil to prevent the noodles from
sticking.

2. In a small bowl, combine the remaining 1 tablespoon of
sesame oil, the soy sauce, vinegar, brown sugar, and peanut
butter, mixing well.

3. Pour the mixture over the noodles then add the carrot,
ginger, scallions, and sesame seeds, tossing to combine.

4. Serve chilled.

Serving Tip

These noodles are perfect for picnics or on-the-go meals as
they can be kept in a cooler until they're served.

CHINESE PORK MEATBALLS

1 pound ground pork
1 tablespoon cornstarch
1 teaspoon minced ginger
3 garlic cloves, minced
2 teaspoons brown sugar
2 teaspoons soy sauce
1 teaspoon five-spice powder
2 pinches ground white pepper
3 tablespoons peanut oil

MAKES 20 MEATBALLS / PREP TIME: 10 MINUTES /
COOK TIME: 10 MINUTES

These meatballs are a slightly different take on the giant pork meatballs so popular in China. They are inspired by Chinese barbecue pork, or *char siew*, and their smaller size means they can be pan-fried in a wok. The five-spice powder infuses the char siew with its unmistakable flavor, and I love charring the outside just a bit for that seared barbecue crispness.

1. In a large bowl, combine the pork, cornstarch, ginger, garlic, brown sugar, soy sauce, five-spice powder, and pepper, and mix well.

2. Roll 1 heaping tablespoon of pork mixture into a ball and continue until all the pork mixture is used.

3. In a wok over medium heat, heat the peanut oil. Using a wok spatula, spread the oil to coat enough of the wok surface to fry about 10 meatballs at a time.

4. Lower the meatballs into the wok in batches. Cook without moving for about 2 minutes, or until the bottoms are cooked through. Use the spatula to carefully rotate the meatballs to cook on the other sides.

5. Keep rotating the meatballs gently until cooked through.

Serving Tip

For a heavenly dipping sauce, combine equal parts low-sodium soy sauce and honey.

SAVORY SCRAMBLED EGG AND CRAB LETTUCE WRAPS

1 head lettuce
4 eggs, lightly beaten
Pinch salt
Pinch ground white pepper
½ teaspoon soy sauce
2 scallions, chopped
3 tablespoons peanut oil
½ cup diced water chestnuts
1 small onion, thinly sliced
¾ cup crabmeat
¼ cup Basic Sambal (page 29)
  (optional)

SERVES 4 TO 6 AS PART OF A MULTICOURSE MEAL /
PREP TIME: 10 MINUTES / COOK TIME: 10 MINUTES

These savory lettuce wraps are so good that I bet you won't be able to eat just one. This is not your typical breakfast scrambled egg. It is perfectly seasoned with soy sauce, salt, and pepper, and features crunchy water chestnuts and onion. Serve this with a bit of sambal for a spicy kick.

1. Wash and separate the lettuce leaves. Chill the lettuce leaves in the refrigerator until just before serving.

2. Put the beaten eggs into a medium bowl. Add the salt, pepper, soy sauce, and scallions to the eggs. Stir gently just to combine.

3. In a wok over medium-high heat, heat the peanut oil.

4. Stir-fry the water chestnuts and onion until the onion is slightly translucent.

5. Add the crabmeat to the wok, then the egg mixture, and let it sit for a moment. When the bottom of the egg is cooked through, flip, and cook on the other side.

6. Using a wok spatula, break up and scramble the egg.

7. Serve with the chilled lettuce leaves and sambal (if using).

Variation Tip

Omit the crab to make this dish vegetarian. It's delicious!

CHINESE CHICKEN SALAD CUPS

FOR THE CHICKEN CUPS

4 ounces skinless, boneless
   chicken tenderloins
Salt
Pepper
3 tablespoons olive oil, divided
15 to 20 wonton wrappers
1 small head romaine lettuce,
   shredded
1 carrot, julienned
2 scallions, chopped
¼ cup sliced almonds
¼ cup chopped fresh cilantro

FOR THE SALAD DRESSING

4 tablespoons apple
   cider vinegar
2 tablespoons sesame oil
2 tablespoons honey

MAKES 15 TO 20 CUPS / PREP TIME: 20 MINUTES /
COOK TIME: 8 MINUTES

These tasty cups are sure to be a big hit at your next party.
A delicious, crunchy chicken salad tossed in an apple cider
vinaigrette, served in a crispy wonton cup—how can you
resist? You can use any type of chicken for this dish, but my
favorite is chicken tenderloins because they crumble easily
to blend into the salad. For a vegetarian version, simply leave
out the chicken.

1. Season the chicken tenderloins with salt and pepper. In a
wok over medium heat, heat 1 tablespoon of olive oil. Add
the chicken and sear on both sides until cooked through,
about 1 minute per side. Remove the chicken from the wok
and chop it finely.

2. Preheat the oven to 375°F.

3. Brush each wonton wrapper on both sides with a
thin layer of olive oil. Arrange the wonton wrappers in
a regular-size muffin pan to form little cups.

4. Bake the wrappers for 6 minutes. Allow them to cool
completely.

5. While the wrappers are baking, make the salad dressing. Combine the apple cider vinegar, sesame oil, and honey in a small bowl, and mix well.

6. In a large bowl, combine the chicken, lettuce, carrot, scallions, almonds, and cilantro with the salad dressing and toss well.

7. Fill each wonton cup with the salad and serve.

Variation Tip

Brush the wonton skins with oil, cut them into ½-inch strips, then bake for about 5 minutes. Arrange the wonton strips over the top of the salad, and serve the salad in a big family-style bowl as opposed to individual cups.

Hot and Sour Soup, page 46

Soups

EGG DROP SOUP

1½ tablespoons cornstarch

3 tablespoons water

4 cups Basic Chinese Chicken Stock (page 25), or store bought

1 teaspoon salt

2 eggs, lightly beaten

1 medium tomato, diced

Pinch ground white pepper

1 scallion, chopped

SERVES: 4 / PREP TIME: 10 MINUTES / COOK TIME: 10 MINUTES

Egg drop soup, also known as egg flower soup, has become a mainstay in Chinese restaurants across the United States. Each restaurant has its own take, but at its core, it's essentially thickened chicken stock mixed with silky beaten egg and garnished with scallions. Simple, yet so tasty and soothing. Basic Chinese chicken stock works best for this recipe, but you can also use store-bought chicken stock in a pinch.

1. In a small bowl, combine the cornstarch and water.

2. In a wok over medium-high heat, bring the chicken stock to a boil. Add the salt.

3. Stir in the cornstarch-water mixture. Return to a boil.

4. Using a pair of chopsticks, swirl the soup, and at the same time slowly pour the beaten eggs into the soup. Swirl faster for a thinner, silky consistency; or slower for a thicker, chunky egg consistency.

5. Add the tomato and pepper, stir, and simmer for 1 minute.

6. Garnish with the scallion, and serve.

Healthy Cooking Tip

Use only egg whites to reduce the cholesterol content. If you don't mind a slightly thinner soup, reduce or omit the cornstarch for a lower carb count. Add some diced tofu for additional protein.

LOTUS ROOT WITH PORK RIBS SOUP

1 pound pork ribs, cut into
  1-inch pieces

1 pound lotus root, peeled and
  cut into ¼-inch-thick rounds

½ teaspoon peppercorns

½ cup dried red dates
  (optional)

12 cups water

2 tablespoons soy sauce

1 teaspoon salt

¼ cup dried goji berries

SERVES 6 TO 8 / PREP TIME: 10 MINUTES /
COOK TIME: 4 HOURS

This combination of lotus root and pork ribs is a classic and
nutritious Chinese soup. It takes a while to cook, but this
one is really worth the wait—the flavor is truly phenomenal.
The pork ribs are fall-off-the-bone tender and the lotus root
remains just slightly crunchy.

1. Place the pork ribs, lotus root, peppercorns, red dates
(if using), and water in a wok.

2. Simmer over low heat for at least 4 hours, and up to
6 hours.

3. Turn off the heat and add the soy sauce, salt, and goji
berries.

4. Allow the soup to sit for about 15 minutes for the goji
berries to reconstitute, then serve.

Cooking Tip

Use a good, sharp cleaver to cut the pork ribs into 1-inch
pieces, or ask your butcher to cut the pork ribs for you.
Leaving them whole is fine as well. Alternatively, you can
use pork shoulder for this recipe.

HOT AND SOUR SOUP

6 cups Basic Chinese Chicken Stock (page 25), or store bought

4 tablespoons water

2 tablespoons cornstarch

2 tablespoons soy sauce

1 teaspoon dark soy sauce

¼ cup rice vinegar or apple cider vinegar

2 teaspoons sesame oil

2 teaspoons brown sugar

2 pinches ground white pepper

2 teaspoons Sichuan chili oil

½ cup diced firm tofu

4 large shiitake mushrooms, soaked then cut into thin strips

½ cup dried wood ear mushrooms, soaked and cut into thin strips

¼ cup sliced bamboo shoots

2 eggs, lightly beaten

SERVES 6 TO 8 / PREP TIME: 10 MINUTES / COOK TIME: 10 MINUTES

Hot and sour soup is my soup of choice at restaurants in the United States. If you love the flavor but don't like the spice, simply leave out the chili oil. If you like it extra spicy, replace the chili oil with red pepper flakes.

1. In a wok over medium-high heat, bring the chicken stock to a boil.

2. Combine the water and cornstarch in a small bowl and set it aside.

3. Add the soy sauce, dark soy sauce, vinegar, sesame oil, brown sugar, white pepper, and chili oil.

4. Add the tofu, shiitake mushrooms, wood ear mushrooms, and bamboo shoots. Bring to a boil.

5. While stirring, slowly add the cornstarch mixture. Return to a boil.

6. Use chopsticks to stir the soup while slowly pouring the beaten eggs into the soup. The faster you swirl and the faster you pour, the silkier the egg. Swirl and pour slowly for a chunkier egg texture.

Better Than Takeout

One cup of hot and sour soup at P.F. Chang's has 1,440 milligrams sodium—over half the daily sodium intake recommended by the Food and Drug Administration. One cup of this recipe, on the other hand, contains nearly half as much sodium: only 754 milligrams!

WATERCRESS AND PORK SOUP

12 cups water, divided

½ pound pork ribs or
pork shoulder, cut into
1-inch pieces

6 to 10 dried red dates

¼ cup dried goji berries

1 pound watercress

1 tablespoon salt

3 pinches ground white pepper

SERVES 6 TO 8 / PREP TIME: 10 MINUTES /
COOK TIME: 4 HOURS

Most vegetables have great nutritional value, but watercress gets superfood status for its abundance of antioxidants and cancer-fighting properties. In Chinese cuisine you'll find watercress used mostly in soups. Botanically related to wasabi and mustard, watercress has a peppery taste; cooking it in a soup greatly reduces the zesty flavor and leaves just the nice mellow flavors that pair exceptionally well with pork.

1. In a wok, bring 2 cups of water to a boil. Blanch the pork for about 5 minutes. Rinse the pork and the wok, and set the pork aside.

2. In the wok, bring the remaining 10 cups of water to a boil.

3. Return the pork to the wok. Reduce the heat to low and simmer, partially covered, for 3½ hours.

4. Add the red dates, goji berries, watercress, salt, and pepper. Simmer for 10 more minutes, and serve.

Cooking Tip

Blanching the pork results in a clearer soup.

CHICKEN AND SWEET CORN SOUP

2 (14.75-ounce) cans
    cream-style sweet corn
8 cups Basic Chinese Chicken
    Stock (page 25)
    or store bought
2 cups cooked
    shredded chicken
1 teaspoon salt
1 teaspoon sesame oil
3 teaspoons cornstarch mixed
    with 2 tablespoons water
    (optional)
2 eggs, lightly beaten
1 scallion, chopped

SERVES 6 TO 8 / PREP TIME: 10 MINUTES /
COOK TIME: 10 MINUTES

If you're looking to jazz up your Egg Drop Soup (page 44), this soup is the perfect solution. It has the same base as the egg drop soup, but with a hint of sweetness from the corn. You can add other vegetables such as carrot, broccoli, diced tomato, or diced water chestnuts.

1. In a wok over high heat, add the corn to the chicken stock and bring to a boil.

2. Add the shredded chicken, salt, and sesame oil. Return to a boil.

3. Stir in the cornstarch mixture (if using) to thicken the soup. Return to a boil.

4. Use chopsticks to stir the soup and while stirring, pour the beaten eggs into the soup. The faster you swirl and the faster you pour, the silkier the egg. Swirl and pour slowly for a chunkier egg texture.

5. Garnish with the chopped scallion just before serving.

Ingredient Tip

You can use any kind of leftover cooked chicken for this dish as long as it doesn't have any strong sauces on it (like barbecue sauce, etc.). If you are using Chinese chicken stock for this recipe, use the thigh and drumstick meat from the chicken for this soup.

CABBAGE AND PORK MEATBALL SOUP

FOR THE PORK MEATBALLS

½ pound ground pork
¼ pound minced shrimp
  (4 to 6 large shrimp)
¼ cup finely diced water
  chestnuts
1 teaspoon soy sauce
½ teaspoon sugar
½ teaspoon salt
Pinch ground white pepper
1½ tablespoons cornstarch

FOR THE SOUP

10 cups Basic Chinese Chicken
  Stock (page 25), or
  store bought
½ head napa cabbage, cut into
  1-inch pieces
1 carrot, sliced
2 teaspoons salt
2 teaspoons sesame oil
2 teaspoons soy sauce

SERVES 8 TO 10 / PREP TIME: 15 MINUTES, PLUS 15 MINUTES
TO MARINATE / COOK TIME: 35 MINUTES

With light, airy meatballs in a flavorful broth, this soup
complements any Chinese meal. The minced water chestnut
in the meatballs gives every bite a nice crunch. Serve with
vermicelli or glass noodles for a complete meal. It's perfect
for cold weather, but can be enjoyed in any season.

TO MAKE THE MEATBALLS

1. In a bowl, mix the ground pork, shrimp, water chestnuts,
soy sauce, sugar, salt, pepper, and cornstarch. Set aside to
marinate for about 15 minutes.

TO MAKE THE SOUP

1. In a wok over high heat, bring the chicken stock to a boil.

2. Add the cabbage and carrot, and simmer for about
30 minutes.

3. Roll about 1 heaping tablespoon of pork mixture into a
ball and continue until all the pork mixture is used. Carefully drop the meatballs into the boiling soup one at a time.
Avoid stirring. As the meatballs cook, they will rise to the
top. They will take about 3 minutes to cook through.

4. Add the salt, sesame oil, and soy sauce just before
turning off the heat.

Variation Tips

Wok-fry the meatballs before adding them to your soup
for a different texture and flavor. Also, a few dried shiitake
mushrooms will add a luxurious essence to the soup.

SWEET PEANUT SOUP

½ pound raw peanuts,
  shelled and skinned
1 tablespoon baking soda
8 cups water, plus more
  for soaking
4 tablespoons sugar

SERVES 4 TO 6 / PREP TIME: 5 MINUTES, PLUS 10 TO 26 HOURS
INACTIVE / COOK TIME: 2 HOURS

In Asian cuisine, some soups are served for dessert or as
an afternoon delicacy. This soup features a sweet broth
with whole peanuts that melt in your mouth when you
bite into them. A little advance planning yields a special,
tasty soup.

1. Soak the peanuts in a bowl of water overnight.

2. Rinse the peanuts, sprinkle them with the baking soda,
then cover in fresh water to soak for 1 to 2 more hours.

3. Thoroughly rinse the peanuts.

4. In a wok over high heat, bring the 8 cups of water
to a boil.

5. Add the peanuts to the boiling water, reduce the heat to
low, and simmer, partially covered, for 2 hours.

6. Add the sugar in increments until the soup reaches your
desired sweetness.

7. Serve the soup at room temperature, hot, or cold, with
an almond or butter cookie, if desired.

Ingredient Tip

If you can only find raw peanuts with the skins on, you can
easily remove the skins after soaking them overnight. Use
your palms to rub the skin off the peanuts, then simply rinse
them off.

CHINESE MUSHROOM SOUP

1 tablespoon olive oil

½ onion, sliced

2 garlic cloves, minced

1 carrot, cut into thin slices

4 or 5 large shiitake
  mushrooms, cut into
  thin slices

5 or 6 white or brown button
  mushrooms, cut into
  thin slices

1 small bunch enoki
  mushrooms, roots removed

8 cups vegetable stock

¼ cup dried goji berries

2 teaspoons sesame oil

1 tablespoon soy sauce

1 teaspoon salt

SERVES 6 TO 8 / PREP TIME: 10 MINUTES /
COOK TIME: 25 MINUTES

There are three different kinds of mushrooms in this recipe—shiitake, button, and enoki—but you can use any kind of mushroom available at your local farmers' market or grocery store. Stir-frying the vegetables and mushrooms before adding the stock gives this healthy soup a unique and complex flavor.

1. In a wok over medium heat, heat the olive oil.

2. Sauté the onion and garlic until the onion turns slightly translucent.

3. Add the carrot, shiitake mushrooms, button mushrooms, and enoki mushrooms. Sauté for about 1 minute.

4. Pour in the vegetable stock and bring to a boil.

5. Add the goji berries, sesame oil, soy sauce, and salt.

6. Simmer over low heat for about 20 minutes before serving.

Ingredient Tip

Dried shiitake mushrooms are sometimes easier to find than fresh ones. If you are using dried shiitakes, soak them in boiling water for 30 minutes to reconstitute them before slicing.

WONTON SOUP

¼ pound ground pork
¼ pound shrimp,
    peeled, deveined, and
    roughly chopped
1 teaspoon cornstarch
1 teaspoon sesame oil
1 teaspoon soy sauce
½ teaspoon salt
Pinch ground white pepper
20 to 25 square wonton
    wrappers

FOR THE SOUP

8 cups Basic Chinese Chicken
    Stock (page 25), or
    store bought
2 tablespoons low-sodium
    soy sauce
2 teaspoons sesame oil
3 pinches ground white pepper
1 scallion, chopped

SERVES 6 TO 8 / PREP TIME: 20 MINUTES /
COOK TIME: 10 MINUTES

The wontons are very easy to make in this simple yet thoroughly satisfying soup. This Chinese classic is usually served as an appetizer or side dish, but you can make it a complete meal by adding egg noodles and some bok choy.

TO MAKE THE WONTONS

1. In a bowl, mix together the pork, shrimp, cornstarch, sesame oil, soy sauce, salt, and pepper.

2. Place about 1 teaspoon of pork mixture in the center of a wonton wrapper.

3. Dampen your finger with water and run it along the edge of the wonton to help seal it, then fold the wonton in half into a triangle. Gently press the edges to seal.

4. Fold the bottom two corners (just outside the meat filling) toward each other, and press those corners together to seal them. Set the wontons aside.

1. Bring the chicken stock to a boil in a wok over high heat. Add the soy sauce and sesame oil.

2. Bring a separate pot of water to a boil. Carefully drop the wontons into the boiling water.

3. As soon as the wontons are cooked, they will float to the top. When they all float to the top, continue boiling for 2 minutes to cook them all the way through.

4. Using a skimmer, carefully transfer the wontons from the water to the chicken stock.

5. Add the pepper and scallion just before serving.

Cooking Tip

Instead of folding the wontons into triangles, then joining the two bottom corners, you can gather up all four corners of the wonton wrapper and pinch them together just above the filling so they form what look like little coin purses. This coin purse method is slightly easier, but you must allow a few more minutes of boiling time for the bunched dough to cook all the way through.

Bok Choy with Garlic and Ginger, page 72

Vegetables & Tofu

Cooking with Vegetables and Tofu

In contrast to the Western penchant for cold, raw salads, most Chinese vegetable dishes are cooked, allowing for enhanced natural flavors and an added complexity. Whether you like them cold or hot, vegetables are a critical part of any healthy diet. They contain key vitamins and minerals, and possess amazing protective properties against a range of diseases. Definitely worth exploring!

BUYING AND STORING FRESH VEGETABLES

For optimum freshness, try to buy vegetables as close to the source as possible. Your local farmers' market is a good place to find great and often unique produce while supporting local businesses. When choosing vegetables, make sure that they look fresh and crisp with few or no blemishes. Leafy greens should be a dark yet vibrant green, not yellowish.

Most vegetables (especially leafy ones) have a short shelf life, so try not to buy them too far in advance if you don't plan on cooking them soon. Harder vegetables such as carrots last a little longer, so you can store them in your refrigerator for up to 3 weeks.

PREPARING AND CUTTING VEGETABLES

It bears repeating that cutting vegetables into pieces roughly the same size is important so they cook evenly. Otherwise, the smaller pieces will be overcooked and mushy, and the larger pieces will be undercooked and too hard.

LEAFY GREENS: Here's a trick to boost the freshness of leafy greens: About one hour before cooking, soak them in a large bowl of cool tap water to help crisp them up, even if they have already wilted a little. You'll be amazed at how much fresher and crisper they become. Wash and soak leafy greens prior to cutting. To cut, lay each stalk horizontally across a cutting board, then cut vertically into about to 1½-inch pieces. I usually take the greens out of the water and cut them just before I toss them in the wok, while they are still a little wet; the water will help steam them and speed up the cooking time.

CARROTS FOR STIR-FRY: I love cutting carrots into little flower-shaped slices—they look so pretty! Wash and peel the carrot, then cut it in half horizontally so that you have two cylindrical shapes. Cut small grooves along the length of each half, about 1 centimeter apart from one another. Finally, cut the carrot into thin slices.

BROCCOLI FLORETS: Wash and soak the broccoli heads prior to cutting them into florets (or little trees, as my sons would call them). Use a small knife to cut out large florets from

After cutting the carrot in half, cut a small groove along the length.

Cut three or four additional grooves, spacing them evenly.

Cut the carrot into even, thin flower-shaped slices.

the large broccoli stem. Cut them further into bite-size florets by cutting the stem, then pulling them apart.

COOKING ORDER FOR STIR-FRYING

In most cases, a stir-fry begins with garlic and/or ginger to help flavor the oil. Add the vegetables to the wok in the order of their cooking times, from slowest to fastest. Harder vegetables come first, followed by softer leafy greens. This will help ensure an evenly cooked dish.

BUYING TOFU

At the grocery store, you will find several different types of tofu textures ranging from silken to super firm. The softer the tofu, the more water it contains. Firmer tofu contains less water, which gives it much more texture. The water in softer tofu makes for a silkier texture.

The tofu you select depends on the type of dish you are preparing, as well as personal preference. For stir-frying, a firmer tofu is a better option as it can withstand being tossed around in the wok without breaking apart too easily.

If you use soft tofu in a wok, try to refrain from stirring it around. If you stir it too much, it will disintegrate and become part of the sauce! Put the whole block of soft tofu in the wok, use your wok spatula to break it up into several very large pieces, and handle it gently for the rest of the cooking time.

Now let's get to cooking those veggies!

CHINESE BROCCOLI WITH OYSTER SAUCE

2 tablespoons peanut oil

4 garlic cloves, peeled and halved

½ (2-inch) piece ginger, peeled and julienned

1 pound Chinese broccoli (kai lan), rinsed and cut into bite-size pieces

2 tablespoons oyster sauce

1 teaspoon sugar

Pinch ground white pepper

SERVES 6 TO 8 AS PART OF A MULTICOURSE MEAL /
PREP TIME: 5 MINUTES / COOK TIME: 5 MINUTES

Like most kids, when I was little I was not a huge fan of vegetables and tried to avoid them as much as possible. I remember my aunt dragging me to a vegetarian restaurant and ordering as many kinds of vegetables as possible in an attempt to "train" my taste buds to like veggies. That very day, as soon as I tried the *kai lan,* or Chinese broccoli, I was hooked for life. It's tasty and crunchy and pairs perfectly with the oyster sauce.

1. In a wok over medium heat, heat the peanut oil.

2. Add the garlic. As soon as it starts to turn golden brown, add the ginger and give it all a quick stir.

3. Increase the heat to high and immediately add the kai lan, oyster sauce, sugar, and pepper.

4. Stir the kai lan well. Add a tablespoon or two of water to help steam it, if desired.

5. When the kai lan turns bright green and softens a little, remove it from the heat and serve immediately.

Substitution Tip

If Chinese broccoli is not available, you can substitute broccoli rabe or broccolini, or even bok choy.

Variation Tip

Instead of stir-frying the kai lan, leave them whole and blanch them (see page 15) for 2 to 3 minutes. Stir-fry the other ingredients, then drizzle the sauce over the blanched vegetables.

MIXED VEGETABLE STIR-FRY

1 tablespoon peanut oil

1 zucchini, cut into bite-size pieces

1 carrot, thinly sliced

½ pound fresh snow peas, trimmed and strings removed

2 garlic cloves, minced

4 to 6 large mushrooms, quartered

3 tablespoons All-Purpose Stir-Fry Sauce (page 26)

½ teaspoon toasted sesame seeds

SERVES 4 TO 6 AS PART OF A MULTICOURSE MEAL /
PREP TIME: 10 MINUTES / COOK TIME: 5 MINUTES

This recipe is as versatile as it gets, so mix it up! You can use just about any vegetable in this stir-fry so it's a great opportunity to use up those leftover vegetables in the refrigerator. If you have a jar of stir-fry sauce on hand, you can have dinner on the table in 15 minutes.

1. In a wok over medium-high heat, heat the peanut oil.

2. Add the zucchini and carrot, and stir-fry for about 1 minute.

3. When the zucchini and carrot are almost soft, add the snow peas.

4. When the snow peas turn bright green, add the garlic and mushrooms. Stir-fry until the mushrooms start to soften a little.

5. Drizzle in the stir-fry sauce, give it a quick stir to combine, and remove from the heat. Place in a serving dish and serve.

Cooking Tip

Stick with 3 or 4 types of vegetables to keep the dish simple and clean. Choose vegetables with a variety of textures, but always include at least one super-crunchy option such as carrots or water chestnuts.

MA PO TOFU

FOR THE SAUCE

1 teaspoon black bean paste
1 teaspoon spicy bean paste
1 teaspoon soy sauce
1 teaspoon oyster sauce
Pinch ground black pepper
2 teaspoons cornstarch
¼ cup water
½ teaspoon sugar

FOR THE STIR-FRY

1 tablespoon peanut oil
2 garlic cloves, minced
½ pound ground pork
1 package firm tofu, cut into
   1- to 1½-inch cubes
1 scallion, chopped

SERVES 4 AS PART OF A MULTICOURSE MEAL /
PREP TIME: 10 MINUTES / COOK TIME: 15 MINUTES

Ma Po Tofu is one of the most popular Sichuan dishes. The flavor of the tofu and savory pork cooked in spicy bean sauce is a tangy delight. Paired with steamed rice, it makes for heavenly comfort food.

1. In a small bowl, prepare the sauce by mixing together the black bean paste, spicy bean paste, soy sauce, oyster sauce, black pepper, cornstarch, water, and sugar. Set it aside.

2. In a wok over medium-high heat, heat the peanut oil.

3. Stir-fry the garlic and ground pork until the pork is fully cooked.

4. Add the sauce and stir well.

5. When the sauce starts to thicken, add the tofu. Give it a gentle quick stir, taking care not to break the tofu.

6. Remove from the heat and transfer to a serving plate.

7. Garnish with the chopped scallion.

Substitution Tip

The ground pork can be swapped out for ground beef. For a vegetarian version, use diced water chestnuts and mushrooms in place of the ground meat.

Better Than Takeout

This Ma Po Tofu recipe contains 872 milligrams of sodium and 3 grams of carbohydrates per serving, significantly less than you'd get at P.F. Chang's, where the same serving size gives you 1035 milligrams of sodium and 15 milligrams of carbs.

STIR-FRIED TOMATO AND EGGS

4 eggs
Pinch salt
Pinch pepper
1 teaspoon Shaoxing wine
2 tablespoons peanut oil
2 medium tomatoes,
  cut into wedges
½ teaspoon sugar
1 scallion, cut into
  1-inch pieces

SERVES 4 TO 6 AS PART OF A MULTICOURSE MEAL /
PREP TIME: 5 MINUTES / COOK TIME: 5 MINUTES

Most Chinese people grow up eating stir-fried tomato and eggs, so this dish brings back childhood memories and continues to be a staple in the Chinese home kitchen. You'll have to try it to see how delicious it is.

1. In a medium bowl, add the eggs and the Shaoxing wine. Season them with the salt and pepper and beat together until well combined.

2. In a wok over medium-high heat, heat the peanut oil.

3. Pour the egg mixture into the wok and allow the bottom to cook before gently scrambling.

4. Just before the egg starts to cook all the way through, remove it from the wok.

5. Toss the tomato wedges into the wok and stir-fry until they become a little soft.

6. Return the scrambled eggs to the wok with the tomato, then sprinkle the sugar over the stir-fry.

7. Turn off the heat, add the scallion, and give one last stir before transferring to a serving plate.

Ingredient Tip

Choose ripe, softer tomatoes that will break down and release all their yummy juices into the scrambled eggs.

BABY ROMAINE WITH GOJI BERRIES

2 heads baby romaine lettuce

1 tablespoon olive oil

2 garlic cloves, minced

¼ cup dried goji berries

1 teaspoon chicken stock
granules (see page 6)

Pinch salt

2 teaspoons Shaoxing wine

SERVES 4 TO 6 AS PART OF A MULTICOURSE MEAL /
PREP TIME: 5 MINUTES / COOK TIME: 5 MINUTES

It may seem odd to some to hear of romaine lettuce being
stir-fried, but the Chinese do prefer their vegetables cooked
rather than raw, and this applies to lettuce, too! The flavor is
completely transformed, yet the texture remains crisp. Goji
berries give this dish a nutritious and colorful boost.

1. Separate the romaine leaves, rinse them, and drain well.

2. In a wok over high heat, heat the olive oil.

3. Add the garlic, followed by the lettuce leaves, goji
berries, chicken stock granules, salt, and Shaoxing wine,
stirring occasionally.

4. Give all the ingredients a quick stir. Transfer to a serving
plate and serve immediately.

Cooking Tip

Make sure all your ingredients are lined up and ready to go
in order to keep the lettuce somewhat crisp—it will cook in
less than a minute!

Substitution Tip

Regular romaine lettuce works just fine if you can't find baby
romaine. Other crunchy lettuce varieties, such as iceberg,
also work quite well.

STIR-FRIED SPINACH WITH GARLIC

1 tablespoon olive oil

4 garlic cloves, thinly sliced or minced

6 cups fresh spinach, rinsed

Pinch salt

½ teaspoon chicken stock granules (see page 6)

SERVES 4 AS PART OF A MULTICOURSE MEAL / PREP TIME: 5 MINUTES / COOK TIME: 5 MINUTES

Spinach is one of the most nutritious vegetables available throughout the year. It contains iron, antioxidants, and vitamins. It is also delicious when stir-fried with garlic. This is a regular dish on our table. It takes just a few minutes to prepare, proof that healthy eating can be very easy!

1. In a wok over medium-high heat, heat the olive oil.

2. Add the garlic, and stir-fry until aromatic, just a few seconds.

3. Toss in the spinach, salt, and chicken stock granules.

4. Stir-fry the spinach until the leaves wilt.

5. Transfer to a serving dish.

Ingredient Tip

You can use any type of spinach (baby spinach, Chinese spinach, etc.), or even leafy greens like kale or collard greens.

SPICY DRY-FRIED STRING BEANS

FOR THE SAUCE

1 tablespoon Shaoxing wine
1 teaspoon chili bean sauce
1 teaspoon sesame oil
1 teaspoon sugar
½ teaspoon salt

FOR THE STRING BEANS

1 tablespoon peanut oil
1 pound fresh string
    beans, trimmed
8 dried red chile peppers
½-inch piece ginger, peeled
    and julienned
3 garlic cloves, minced

SERVES 4 TO 6 AS PART OF A MULTICOURSE MEAL /
PREP TIME: 5 MINUTES / COOK TIME: 5 MINUTES

In most restaurants, string beans are deep-fried instead of
dry-fried, so it's healthier to prepare this dish at home. Whenever I have a craving for French fries, I whip up a batch of
these crunchy string beans (also known as green beans), and
the craving is satisfied with this healthier and tastier choice.
One word of advice: this cooking method gets a bit smoky,
so make sure your kitchen is well ventilated!

1. In a small bowl, prepare the sauce by mixing together
the Shaoxing wine, chili bean sauce, sesame oil, sugar,
and salt. Set it aside.

2. In a wok over medium-high heat, heat the peanut oil.

3. As soon as the wok starts to smoke, toss in the green
beans. Stir-fry until they are blistered and bright green,
for about 5 minutes. If they start to burn, reduce the heat
to medium.

4. Add the dried red chiles, ginger, and garlic to the wok. Fry until aromatic, then add the sauce. Stir to combine all the ingredients.

5. Remove from the heat, and transfer to a serving plate.

Substitution Tip

If you love this dish but don't love the spice, replace the chili bean sauce with oyster sauce and omit the dried red chiles.

Better Than Takeout

This is a healthier way to eat string beans than P.F. Chang's Crispy Green Beans, as they are not deep-fried. My recipe has 83 calories per serving, with 42 calories from fat; the restaurant version has 260 calories per serving with 182 calories from fat.

BROCCOLI WITH BRAISED SHIITAKE MUSHROOMS

2 cups dried shiitake
mushrooms
Water for soaking mushrooms

FOR THE SAUCE

¼ cup water, plus
  2 tablespoons for
  cornstarch mixture
¼ cup oyster sauce
1 tablespoon soy sauce
1 teaspoon sugar
2 pinches ground white pepper
2 teaspoons cornstarch

FOR THE BROCCOLI

2 heads broccoli, cut
  into florets
1 tablespoon peanut oil
1 tablespoon sesame oil

SERVES 6 TO 8 AS PART OF A MULTICOURSE MEAL /
PREP TIME: 10 MINUTES, PLUS 30 MINUTES FOR SOAKING /
COOK TIME: 20 MINUTES

The depth of flavor of the shiitake mushrooms pairs beautifully with the broccoli in this dish. You can use other types of mushroom, or a combination of different mushrooms, but the flavor of the shiitake and oyster sauce are made for each other.

1. Soak the shiitake mushrooms in water for a few hours or overnight until soft. If pressed for time, boil them in water for 30 minutes.

2. Rinse the mushrooms well, remove their stems, and squeeze as much water out of them as possible. Set them aside.

3. In a small bowl, prepare the sauce by combining ¼ cup of water and the oyster sauce, soy sauce, sugar, and pepper. Set it aside.

4. In another small bowl, combine 2 tablespoons of water and the cornstarch. Set it aside.

5. On a metal steaming rack in a wok over high heat, steam the broccoli florets for 5 minutes. Set them aside, and discard the water from the wok.

6. Return the wok to the stove top. Allow the wok to dry completely. Over medium-low heat, heat the peanut oil and sesame oil.

7. Add the sauce and mushrooms to the wok. Simmer for about 10 minutes, stirring occasionally.

8. Increase the heat to high, and add the cornstarch-water mixture, stirring to thicken the sauce.

9. Put the broccoli on a round serving plate in a circle along the edge. Pour the mushrooms and sauce in the center of the plate, and serve.

HAPPY FAMILY

1 cup thin strips chicken breast

2 teaspoons soy sauce

2 teaspoons cornstarch

2 tablespoons peanut oil

6 to 8 large shrimp

2 garlic cloves, minced

2 cups broccoli florets

1 carrot, sliced

1 cup snow peas, trimmed

1 cup baby corn

1 cup sliced button mushrooms

¼ cup bamboo shoots

¼ cup water chestnuts, sliced

1 cup Brown Sauce (page 28)

SERVES 6 AS PART OF A MULTICOURSE MEAL /
PREP TIME: 5 MINUTES, PLUS 20 MINUTES TO MARINATE /
COOK TIME: 30 MINUTES

Happy Family is a Chinese-American dish that I had never heard of until I moved to the United States. Its name describes how the different ingredients blend together to create a harmonious combination.

1. Marinate the chicken breast strips in the soy sauce and cornstarch for 20 minutes at room temperature.

2. In a wok over medium-high heat, heat the peanut oil.

3. Add the chicken and stir-fry until cooked, then remove the chicken from the wok.

4. Add the shrimp and stir-fry until they are pink and opaque, then remove them from the wok.

5. Toss the garlic into the wok and add the vegetables one by one, stir-frying each for 20 to 30 seconds before adding the next vegetable. Begin with the broccoli, followed by the carrot, snow peas, baby corn, mushrooms, bamboo shoots, and water chestnuts.

6. Return the chicken and shrimp to the wok.

7. Pour in the brown sauce and stir all the ingredients well. As soon as the sauce has thickened, turn off the heat and transfer to a serving plate.

Variation Tip

The ingredients listed here are typical findings in a Happy Family dish at a Chinese restaurant. Feel free to experiment with different types of vegetables and proteins. Use scallops instead of shrimp, or enoki mushrooms instead of button. Add some tofu or tofu skin. So many possibilities! It can also be easily transformed into a vegetarian dish.

SPICY GARLIC EGGPLANT

FOR THE SAUCE

2 tablespoons soy sauce

1½ tablespoons Chinese black vinegar or apple cider vinegar

1 teaspoon dark soy sauce

1½ teaspoons brown sugar

2 teaspoons chili bean paste

FOR THE STIR-FRY

2 Chinese or Japanese eggplant, cut into bite-size pieces

1 teaspoon cornstarch

3 tablespoons peanut oil

4 garlic cloves, minced

1 scallion, chopped

**SERVES 4 AS PART OF A MULTICOURSE MEAL /
PREP TIME: 10 MINUTES / COOK TIME: 10 MINUTES**

Eggplant is an easy ingredient to cook if you know some tricks, and this cooking method is foolproof—it comes out perfect each time. No more soggy eggplant soaked in oil! The spiciness in the luscious sauce can be adjusted according to your taste. If you don't like it spicy, simply omit the chili bean paste.

1. In a small bowl, prepare the sauce by mixing together the soy sauce, vinegar, dark soy sauce, brown sugar, and chili bean paste. Set it aside.

2. Dust the eggplant with a light layer of cornstarch.

3. In a wok over medium-high heat, heat the peanut oil.

4. Stir-fry the eggplant until cooked almost all the way through.

5. Add the garlic and stir-fry until aromatic.

6. Add the sauce to the wok, stir-frying until all the ingredients are mixed, then remove from the heat.

7. Transfer the eggplant to a serving dish, and garnish with the chopped scallion.

STIR-FRIED BEAN SPROUTS

1 tablespoon peanut oil
1 garlic clove, minced
½ carrot, julienned
4 cups fresh mung bean
   sprouts, rinsed
2 teaspoons soy sauce
¼ cup chopped garlic chives
   (1-inch pieces)
Pinch ground white pepper

SERVES 4 TO 6 AS PART OF A MULTICOURSE MEAL /
PREP TIME: 5 MINUTES / COOK TIME: 5 MINUTES

Mung bean sprouts take center stage in this simple, healthy dish. It complements any Chinese dish perfectly in a family-style dinner. By lightly and quickly stir-frying the bean sprouts over high heat, their crispness is maintained and they take on an amazing flavor.

1. In a wok over high heat, heat the peanut oil.

2. Add the garlic and stir-fry for just a few seconds until aromatic.

3. Add the carrot and stir-fry for 2 or 3 seconds.

4. Toss the bean sprouts into the wok, followed by the soy sauce. Stir well for a few seconds then turn off the heat.

5. Add the garlic chives and pepper at the last minute, and transfer to a serving bowl.

Substitution Tip

If you are not able to find garlic chives, you can use scallions instead.

BOK CHOY WITH GARLIC AND GINGER

1 tablespoon olive oil

2 garlic cloves, thinly sliced
   or minced

1-inch piece ginger, peeled
   and julienned

4 heads bok choy, cut into
   bite-size pieces

1 tablespoon Shaoxing wine

½ teaspoon chicken stock
   granules (see page 6)

¼ teaspoon salt

SERVES 4 TO 6 AS PART OF A MULTICOURSE MEAL /
PREP TIME: 5 MINUTES / COOK TIME: 5 MINUTES

Bok choy is one of the most nutritious vegetables available all year round. It contains hardly any calories, so you can enjoy as much as you want guilt-free. Garlic and ginger flavor the bok choy. Delicious!

1. Pour the olive oil into a cold wok then add the garlic and ginger.

2. Turn the heat to medium-high. When the garlic starts to brown just a little, add the bok choy and stir-fry for a few seconds.

3. Add the Shaoxing wine, which will help steam the bok choy. Add a little water if needed.

4. Sprinkle the chicken stock granules over the bok choy and stir well.

5. When the stems of the bok choy are tender, they are ready to eat.

Serving Tip

If you are using baby bok choy, cut them in half lengthwise for a stunning presentation.

STRING BEANS WITH GROUND PORK

1 tablespoon oyster sauce

2 teaspoons Shaoxing wine

2 teaspoons soy sauce

1 teaspoon sugar

Pinch ground white pepper

Pinch salt

¼ pound ground pork

1 tablespoon peanut oil

1 pound green beans, trimmed
and cut into 1-inch pieces

2 garlic cloves, minced

SERVES 6 TO 8 AS PART OF A MULTICOURSE MEAL /
PREP TIME: 5 MINUTES, PLUS 20 MINUTES TO MARINATE /
COOK TIME: 5 MINUTES

This dish brings together the crispness of green beans with the savory flavor of marinated pork to create a complex and nutritious feast—all in less time than it takes to order takeout!

1. In a small bowl, mix together the oyster sauce, Shaoxing wine, soy sauce, sugar, pepper, and salt. Pour the mixure over the ground pork, mix to combine, and marinate for 20 minutes.

2. In a wok over medium-high heat, heat the peanut oil.

3. Add the ground pork and stir-fry for about a minute, or until partially cooked. Add the green beans and garlic.

4. Reduce the heat to low, and continue to cook until the green beans have softened, for 2 to 3 minutes, adding water to the wok to help steam the green beans if needed.

5. Remove from the heat and serve.

Serving Tip

Enjoy this with steamed white or brown rice
(pages 20 and 22).

Substitution Tip

Replace the ground pork with ground beef, or with diced shiitake mushrooms for a vegetarian twist.

SIMPLE STIR-FRIED CABBAGE

1½ tablespoons olive oil
2 garlic cloves, minced
1 head cabbage, shredded
1 tablespoon Shaoxing wine
  or water
2 tablespoons soy sauce
Pinch salt
Pinch ground white pepper

SERVES 4 TO 6 AS PART OF A MULTICOURSE MEAL /
PREP TIME: 5 MINUTES / COOK TIME: 5 MINUTES

Stir-fried cabbage is a common side dish in many Chinese households. When I was attending college, I made this dish frequently because it was filling and budget-friendly. Stir-frying gives the cabbage a depth of flavor that will surprise you.

1. In a wok over medium-high heat, heat the olive oil.

2. Add the garlic, stir-fry for about 20 seconds, and add the cabbage.

3. Using a wok spatula, stir the cabbage for about 1 minute, then add the Shaoxing wine, soy sauce, salt, and pepper.

4. Stir-fry until the cabbage has wilted.

5. Remove from the heat and serve.

Variation Tips

For a spicy kick, add red pepper flakes or Sichuan peppercorns when stir-frying the garlic. You can also add ¼ cup of julienned carrot for a touch of sweetness and color.

HOISIN TOFU

SERVES 2 TO 4 AS PART OF A MULTICOURSE MEAL /
PREP TIME: 5 MINUTES / COOK TIME: 5 MINUTES

FOR THE SAUCE

2 tablespoons hoisin sauce

1 tablespoon honey

2 teaspoons sesame oil

1 teaspoon soy sauce

FOR THE STIR-FRY

2 tablespoons peanut oil

1 block firm tofu, cut into
1- to 1½-inch cubes

1 teaspoon toasted
sesame seeds

1 scallion, chopped

Tofu is high in protein and very adaptable to just about any sauce you pair it with. Hoisin sauce, sweetened with honey, sets the tone with its rich flavor. Use firm tofu because it holds up better to stir-frying than the silken variety. Each cube gets coated in the sauce, then topped with toasted sesame seeds and chopped scallions for transcendent flavor and crunch.

1. In a small bowl, make the sauce by combining the hoisin sauce, honey, sesame oil, and soy sauce. Set it aside.

2. In a wok over medium-high heat, heat the peanut oil.

3. Carefully drop the tofu cubes into the wok, and allow the bottom side to cook for about 20 seconds before gently flipping them over.

4. When the tofu is cooked on all sides, top with the sauce, gently stirring to coat the tofu cubes.

5. Transfer the tofu to a serving plate. Garnish with the sesame seeds and chopped scallion.

Serving Tip

I recommend serving this dish with Steamed Brown Rice (page 22). The crunchy brown rice will go nicely with the soft tofu.

Orange Chicken, page 88

Poultry

Cooking with Chicken

Chicken is fairly inexpensive, low in fat, and nutritious. It's no wonder it is so popular around the world, and Chinese cuisine is no exception. Its mild flavor makes it highly adaptable to a limitless array of sauces, spices, and cooking techniques.

BUYING AND STORING CHICKEN

The cuts of chicken you buy might depend greatly on your budget, or how health-conscious you are. In healthy cooking, chicken breast is most commonly used for its low fat content. It doesn't hurt to indulge in the slightly fattier (but juicier and tastier) skinless chicken thighs every once in a while, too. Those are the two most common cuts I purchase for every-day meals.

Raw chicken only keeps in the refrigerator for about 2 days, so plan your meals accordingly. Check the expiration date on the package, and be sure the meat is still pink in color and smells fresh. If you need to store it for more than 2 days, tuck it in the freezer. If you plan on keeping it in your freezer for longer than 1 month, you can double wrap it in freezer-safe bags to prevent freezer burn.

CUTTING AND PREPARING CHICKEN FOR COOKING

Freezing the chicken for about 30 minutes prior to cutting will make it a lot easier to slice and ensure clean, even cuts. A sharp knife helps complete the task with finesse.

Place the chicken on the cutting board with the smooth (outer) side of the chicken facing up. First, trim off any excess fat. Next, cut the chicken lengthwise into thin strips about ¼ inch thick, or into cubes by cutting those strips into smaller pieces. Cutting against the grain will make the meat more tender.

Many Chinese recipes call for the chicken to marinate in cornstarch along with some liquid seasonings—a process called "velveting." Cornstarch is the secret ingredient that keeps the chicken tender when cooked, by creating a barrier against the high heat of the wok and helping to seal in the meat's juices.

Allow chicken to marinate in the cornstarch and seasonings for a maximum of 30 minutes, and always at room temperature unless directed otherwise. Adding chicken to a hot wok straight from the refrigerator will cause it to stick to the wok.

STIR-FRYING CHICKEN

First, check that the wok is hot enough before adding the chicken. There should be just a little bit of smoke coming from the wok. The chicken's temperature matters too—it should be close to room temperature.

Spread the chicken out in one layer in the wok. Allow the bottom to fully cook (this should take 20 to 30 seconds) before flipping or stir-frying. When the chicken is mostly cooked through on all sides, remove it from the wok to prevent overcooking. It will return to the wok later to finish.

Stir-fry the rest of the ingredients (vegetables, etc.), then return the chicken to the wok and give everything a good stir. Add the sauce at the very last minute, just before turning off the heat. This process varies a bit from recipe to recipe, but you'll start to see a formula.

MUSHROOM CHICKEN

FOR THE MARINADE

2 teaspoons soy sauce

½ teaspoon salt

2 pinches ground white pepper

3 teaspoons cornstarch

2 boneless skinless chicken
   breast halves, cut into
   bite-size pieces

FOR THE STIR-FRY

2 tablespoons peanut oil

1 medium zucchini, cut into
   bite-size pieces

1-inch piece ginger, peeled
   and minced

½ pound cremini or button
   mushrooms, cut into
   quarters or slices

½ cup Brown Sauce (page 28)

½ teaspoon toasted
   sesame seeds

SERVES 6 TO 8 AS PART OF A MULTICOURSE MEAL /
PREP TIME: 5 MINUTES, PLUS 20 MINUTES TO MARINATE /
COOK TIME: 5 MINUTES

Mushroom Chicken got its fame from the Panda Express restaurant chain, and is one of their healthier dishes that you can make at home. This easy recipe features tender chicken and fresh, crisp zucchini with delicate button mushrooms in a delicious brown sauce.

1. Pour the soy sauce, salt, pepper, and cornstarch over the chicken breast and toss to combine. Marinate at room temperature for about 20 minutes.

2. In a wok over medium-high heat, heat the peanut oil.

3. Add the chicken and stir-fry until it turns lightly golden brown on all sides. Remove it from the wok and set it aside.

4. Add the zucchini to the wok and stir-fry until slightly tender, then remove it from the wok and set it aside.

5. Add a little more oil to the wok if needed. Add the ginger and stir-fry for about 20 seconds, then add the mushrooms. Stir-fry the mushrooms until slightly brown.

6. Return the chicken and zucchini to the wok with the mushrooms and stir in the brown sauce.

7. When the sauce thickens, transfer the dish to a serving plate. Top with the sesame seeds.

Cooking Tip

The water in the mushrooms will come out as they cook. Spread the mushrooms around the wok to let the water evaporate, so that the mushrooms can cook to golden-brown perfection.

Better Than Takeout

At Panda Express, this dish contains 750 milligrams of sodium per 5.9-ounce serving. Here, the same serving size has 549 milligrams of sodium.

SWEET AND SOUR CHICKEN

2 teaspoons soy sauce

Pinch ground white pepper

2 teaspoons cornstarch

2 (5-ounce) boneless chicken
   breast halves, cut into
   bite-size pieces

2 tablespoons peanut oil

2 garlic cloves, minced

¼ cup Sweet and Sour Sauce
   (page 27)

1 carrot, sliced

1 small onion, cut into wedges

1 red bell pepper, cut into
   1-inch pieces

1 scallion, chopped

SERVES 4 TO 6 AS PART OF A MULTICOURSE MEAL /
PREP TIME: 5 MINUTES, PLUS 20 MINUTES TO MARINATE /
COOK TIME: 5 MINUTES

This is a healthy take on a beloved fast food classic. Most restaurants deep-fry the chicken in so much batter that you end up with more batter than chicken. Here the chicken is stir-fried instead of deep-fried, then coated in a delicious sweet and sour sauce. Just as tasty, and no bellyache!

1. Pour the soy sauce, white pepper, and cornstarch over the chicken breast and toss to combine. Marinate at room temperature for about 20 minutes.

2. In a wok over medium-high heat, heat the peanut oil.

3. Add the chicken and stir-fry until slightly golden brown on all sides. Remove it from the wok and set it aside.

4. Add the garlic and stir-fry for about 20 seconds. Add the sweet and sour sauce, followed by the carrot, onion, and bell pepper.

5. Return the chicken to the wok and mix all the ingredients well. Remove from the heat and transfer to a serving plate. Garnish with the chopped scallion.

Variation Tip

If you absolutely must have deep-fried crispy chicken with your sweet and sour sauce, go ahead and indulge every once in a while—just make it yourself! Instead of coating each piece of chicken with a ton of batter, use a thin layer of cornstarch or tapioca flour.

GINGER CHICKEN

1 teaspoon sesame oil

½ teaspoon salt

Pinch ground white pepper

1 tablespoon cornstarch

2 chicken breast halves, cut
    into bite-size pieces

FOR THE STIR-FRY

1 tablespoon sesame oil

2 tablespoons peanut oil

2-inch piece ginger, peeled
    and thinly sliced

2 tablespoons water

1 teaspoon soy sauce

2 bunches scallions, cut into
    1-inch pieces

SERVES 4 TO 6 AS PART OF A MULTICOURSE MEAL /
PREP TIME: 5 MINUTES, PLUS 20 MINUTES TO MARINATE /
COOK TIME: 5 MINUTES

An essential part of Chinese cooking, the magic plant root called ginger is not just delicious; it also has medicinal benefits—especially for relieving stomach ailments. The ginger in this recipe adds a bold flavor and healthy touch to the velvety sauce.

1. Pour 1 teaspoon of sesame oil, the salt, pepper, and cornstarch over the chicken and toss to coat. Marinate at room temperature for about 20 minutes.

2. In a wok over medium-high heat, heat the peanut oil.

3. Add the chicken and stir-fry in two batches until fully cooked.

4. Remove the chicken from the wok and set it aside.

5. Add the remaining 1 tablespoon of sesame oil to the wok. Add the ginger and stir-fry for about 1 minute.

6. Return the chicken to the wok and add the water and soy sauce. Stir-fry until the sauce thickens a little.

7. Add the scallions, stir well to combine, turn off the heat, and serve.

Serving Tip

Serve this with steamed white or brown rice
(pages 20 and 22) to soak up the velvety sauce.

Substitution Tip

Instead of chicken, try this dish with thinly sliced beef.

SESAME OIL CHICKEN

2 tablespoons sesame oil

2-inch piece ginger, peeled
  and julienned

4 chicken drumsticks
  (bone-in), chopped into
  2 or 3 pieces each

2 tablespoons Shaoxing wine

2 teaspoons soy sauce

¼ teaspoon dark soy sauce

½ cup water

Pinch ground white pepper

SERVES 4 TO 6 AS PART OF A MULTICOURSE MEAL /
PREP TIME: 5 MINUTES / COOK TIME: 10 MINUTES

In Chinese culture, new mothers are served special foods during the first month after childbirth. These foods are chosen for their ability to assist in recovery, rejuvenating the body and expelling toxins. Sesame Oil Chicken is one of these dishes. It's not only nutritious, but also very aromatic and luscious. Enjoy it with steamed white or brown rice (pages 20 and 22).

1. In a wok over medium-high heat, heat the sesame oil.

2. Add the ginger and stir-fry until it turns a very light golden brown.

3. Add the chicken pieces and stir-fry for about 1 minute to cook the surface.

4. Stir in the Shaoxing wine, soy sauce, dark soy sauce, water, and pepper.

5. Stir the chicken well, reduce the heat to low, and simmer until tender, 5 to 10 minutes.

6. Transfer to a serving plate and serve immediately.

Ingredient Tip

Ask a butcher to cut the drumsticks for you, or simply leave them whole. You can also use chicken thighs, chicken wings, or drumettes. The more tender dark meat works best in this recipe—chicken breast might end up too dry.

GENERAL TSO'S CHICKEN

SERVES 4 TO 6 AS PART OF A MULTICOURSE MEAL /
PREP TIME: 5 MINUTES, PLUS 20 MINUTES TO MARINATE /
COOK TIME: 10 MINUTES

FOR THE MARINADE

2 teaspoons cornstarch

¼ teaspoon salt

2 pinches ground white pepper

2 boneless chicken breast
   halves, cut into
   bite-size pieces

FOR THE SAUCE

2 tablespoons ketchup

3 teaspoons rice vinegar

2 teaspoons hoisin sauce

2 teaspoons brown sugar

2 teaspoons soy sauce

FOR THE STIR-FRY

2 tablespoons peanut oil

¼ dried red chile

½ teaspoon toasted
   sesame seeds

1 scallion, chopped

General Tso's Chicken, named after General Zuo Zongtang, is a Hunan dish that became popular in America after it was introduced in the early 1970s. It has been tweaked to suit American tastes, but maintains the classic Hunanese trifecta of spicy, sweet, and salty flavors. Keeping the healthy theme, the chicken is stir-fried as opposed to deep-fried, but no flavor is lost.

1. In a small bowl, mix the cornstarch, salt, and white pepper. Sprinkle over the chicken, tossing to coat, and marinate at room temperature for 20 minutes.

2. Meanwhile, in a separate small bowl, make the sauce by combining the ketchup, rice vinegar, hoisin sauce, brown sugar, and soy sauce, mixing it well. Set the sauce aside.

3. In a wok over medium-high heat, heat the peanut oil.

4. Add the chicken and stir-fry in batches until fully cooked and slightly brown.

5. Add the chile and pour in the sauce. Stir to coat the chicken in the sauce.

6. Turn off the heat and transfer the dish to a serving plate.

7. Garnish with the sesame seeds and chopped scallion.

POULTRY

CHICKEN WITH CASHEW NUTS

2 tablespoons peanut oil

2 garlic cloves, minced

½ onion, thinly sliced

2 boneless skinless chicken
    breast halves, cut into
    thin strips

1½ tablespoons brown sugar

1 tablespoon soy sauce

1 tablespoon oyster sauce

1 teaspoon fish sauce

½ cup cashews, lightly roasted

1 scallion, chopped

SERVES 4 TO 6 AS PART OF A MULTICOURSE MEAL /
PREP TIME: 5 MINUTES / COOK TIME: 10 MINUTES

This dish offers a slight twist on the traditional Chinese cashew chicken. The fish sauce brings an incredible depth of flavor to the plate. Add the crunch of roasted cashews, and this will quickly become one of your family favorites.

1. In a wok over medium heat, heat the peanut oil.

2. Add the garlic and onion and stir-fry until fragrant.

3. Add the chicken and stir-fry until the chicken is almost fully cooked.

4. Combine the brown sugar, soy sauce, oyster sauce, and fish sauce, and add to the chicken.

5. Increase the heat to high, stir well to mix, and continue stirring until the chicken is fully cooked.

6. Stir in the cashew nuts.

7. Garnish with the chopped scallion, and serve.

Serving Tip

Enjoy this with steamed white or brown rice
(pages 20 and 22).

Variation Tip

Add diced celery for extra crunch and a different flavor.

MOO GOO GAI PAN

SERVES 6 TO 8 AS PART OF A MULTICOURSE MEAL /
PREP TIME: 5 MINUTES, PLUS 20 MINUTES TO MARINATE /
COOK TIME: 5 MINUTES

FOR THE MARINADE

2 teaspoons soy sauce

2 pinches ground white pepper

3 tablespoons cornstarch

2 boneless chicken breast
halves, cut into thin strips

FOR THE SAUCE

½ cup Basic Chinese Chicken
Stock (page 25), or
store bought

1 teaspoon rice vinegar

1 teaspoon Shaoxing wine

1 teaspoon cornstarch

½ teaspoon salt

½ teaspoon sugar

FOR THE STIR-FRY

2 tablespoons peanut oil

1-inch piece ginger, peeled
and julienned

2 garlic cloves, minced

2 cups snow peas

4 to 6 button
mushrooms, sliced

¼ cup bamboo shoots

¼ cup water chestnuts, sliced

Moo goo gai pan is a Cantonese dish that means "sliced chicken and mushrooms." This recipe also features vegetables like snow peas, bamboo shoots, and water chestnuts, all in a delicious sauce.

1. Pour the soy sauce, pepper and cornstarch over the chicken then toss to coat. Marinate at room temperature for 20 minutes.

2. In a separate bowl, prepare the sauce by mixing together the chicken stock, rice vinegar, Shaoxing wine, cornstarch, salt, and sugar. Set it aside.

3. In a wok over medium-high heat, heat the peanut oil. Add the chicken to the wok and stir-fry until almost fully cooked. Remove the chicken from the wok and set it aside.

4. Stir-fry the ginger and garlic for about 15 seconds and add the snow peas.

5. When the snow peas start to turn bright green after about 2 minutes, stir in the mushrooms, bamboo shoots, and water chestnuts.

6. When the mushrooms begin to soften, add the sauce and return the chicken to the wok. Stir-fry to combine all the ingredients.

7. When the sauce has thickened after about 20 seconds, transfer the dish to a serving plate.

Variation Tip

The traditional version features a white sauce, but you can also use Brown Sauce (page 28).

POULTRY

ORANGE CHICKEN

FOR THE MARINADE

2 (5-ounce) boneless chicken
   breast halves, cut into
   bite-size pieces
3 teaspoons cornstarch
2 teaspoons soy sauce
2 pinches ground white pepper

FOR THE SAUCE

3 to 4 orange peel strips,
   julienned
2 tablespoons water
2 tablespoons apple
   cider vinegar
1 tablespoon orange juice
2 teaspoons brown sugar
2 teaspoons cornstarch
1 teaspoon soy sauce
½ teaspoon ketchup
2 star anise petals
1 clove
Pinch red pepper flakes

FOR THE STIR-FRY

2 tablespoons peanut oil
1 scallion, chopped
½ teaspoon toasted
   sesame seeds

SERVES 4 TO 6 AS PART OF A MULTICOURSE MEAL /
PREP TIME: 5 MINUTES, PLUS 20 MINUTES TO MARINATE /
COOK TIME: 5 MINUTES

Orange Chicken is a dish from the Hunan province that
has been popularized by the Panda Express fast food chain.
While we thank them, we are keeping things healthy by
stir-frying instead of deep-frying the chicken. The key ingredient is fresh orange peel, which gives the sauce its sweet
and tart flavor.

1. Sprinkle the chicken with the cornstarch, soy sauce, and
pepper and toss to combine. Marinate at room temperature
for 20 minutes.

2. In a small bowl, make the sauce by mixing together
the orange peel, water, apple cider vinegar, orange juice,
brown sugar, cornstarch, soy sauce, ketchup, star anise,
clove, and red pepper flakes. Set it aside.

3. In a wok over medium-high heat, heat the peanut oil.

4. Add the chicken and stir-fry until slightly golden brown. Remove the chicken from the wok and set it aside.

5. Pour the sauce into the wok and stir until it becomes thick.

6. Return the chicken to the wok and stir well to coat each piece.

7. Transfer to a serving plate and garnish with the scallion and sesame seeds.

8. Serve immediately.

Better Than Takeout

While this may be a Panda Express favorite, you're better off making the homemade version. Just consider the difference between a 5-ounce serving of this recipe, which contains 250 calories and 395 milligrams of sodium, and the same serving size of the Panda Express version, which has 380 calories and 620 milligrams of sodium.

HONEY SESAME CHICKEN

FOR THE MARINADE

3 teaspoons cornstarch
1 egg white
½ teaspoon salt
Pinch ground white pepper
2 (5-ounce) boneless chicken
   breast halves

FOR THE SAUCE

2 tablespoons honey
1½ tablespoons apple
   cider vinegar
1 teaspoon soy sauce
½ teaspoon sesame oil
½ teaspoon salt

FOR THE STIR-FRY

2 tablespoons peanut oil
1 teaspoon toasted
   sesame seeds
1 scallion, chopped

SERVES 4 TO 6 AS PART OF A MULTICOURSE MEAL /
PREP TIME: 5 MINUTES, PLUS 2 MINUTES TO MARINATE /
COOK TIME: 5 MINUTES

Satisfy your takeout cravings with this tender chicken smothered in a honey-sesame sauce, perfect over a bowl of steamed rice. Ridiculously easy to make in just 30 minutes and requiring ingredients you probably already have in your kitchen, it is tastier and healthier than takeout.

1. Pour the cornstarch, egg white, salt, and pepper over the chicken and toss to combine. Marinate at room temperature for 20 minutes.

2. In a small bowl, prepare the sauce by mixing together the honey, apple cider vinegar, soy sauce, sesame oil, and salt.

3. In a wok over medium-high heat, heat the peanut oil.

4. Add the chicken and stir-fry until fully cooked.

5. Stir in the sauce, mixing well to coat the chicken.

6. Sprinkle the sesame seeds over the chicken, stirring well.

7. Transfer to a serving dish and top with the scallion.

Cooking Tip

Since honey is very thick and sticky, stir the sauce well before you pour it into the wok. The liquids in the sauce will thin the honey so it pours easily.

BLACK PEPPER CHICKEN
WITH ASPARAGUS

3 teaspoons cornstarch
2 teaspoons Shaoxing wine
½ teaspoon salt
Pinch freshly ground
    black pepper
2 (5-ounce) boneless skinless
    chicken breast halves, cut
    into bite-size pieces

FOR THE SAUCE

1 tablespoon oyster sauce
1 teaspoon rice vinegar
½ teaspoon soy sauce
½ teaspoon dark soy sauce
1 teaspoon freshly ground
    black pepper

FOR THE STIR-FRY

2 tablespoons peanut oil
½ pound asparagus (about
    ½ bunch), stems trimmed,
    cut into 1-inch pieces

SERVES 4 TO 6 AS PART OF A MULTICOURSE MEAL /
PREP TIME: 5 MINUTES, PLUS 20 MINUTES TO MARINATE /
COOK TIME: 5 MINUTES

This quick stir-fry is perfect for even the busiest of week-nights, and it's loaded with flavor! Tender chicken and crisp asparagus in a bold black pepper sauce, served over a warm bowl of steamed rice—not bad for a hectic Tuesday, right?

1. Pour the cornstarch, Shaoxing wine, salt, and pepper over the chicken and toss to combine. Marinate at room temperature for 20 minutes.

2. In a small bowl, prepare the sauce by combining the oyster sauce, rice vinegar, soy sauce, dark soy sauce, and pepper, and mix it well. Set it aside.

3. In a wok over medium-high heat, heat the peanut oil.

4. Add the chicken and stir-fry until the chicken is half cooked.

5. Add the asparagus and stir-fry until it turns bright green and the chicken is fully cooked, or for about 2 minutes.

6. Add the sauce to the wok, and stir well to combine all the ingredients.

7. Transfer to a serving dish and serve.

Serving Tip

This dish is great with steamed white or brown rice (pages 20 and 22).

Pork Ribs with Black Bean Sauce, page 102

Pork & Beef

Cooking with Pork and Beef

Pork is by far the most popular meat in China. It is highly versatile and lends a great deal of flavor to a dish. Pork can be grilled, stir-fried, deep-fried, roasted, steamed, or stewed with excellent results.

In China, beef is more expensive than pork so it is not used as widely, but its popularity has soared in recent years. In most Chinese dishes, beef is cut into thin strips, then stir-fried or deep-fried. It's also used in soups and stews.

Both meats are high in protein and can be low in fat if the right cuts are used.

BUYING AND STORING MEAT

Raw beef and pork last only 3 to 4 days in the refrigerator—even less if it's ground meat—so it's a good strategy to shop knowing what meals you will be preparing so you can purchase the best cuts for those dishes.

PORK: The color of good fresh pork should be pink to a darker red. Stay away from the very pale pink to white cuts as they seldom have any flavor.

BEEF: Look for a bright red color. Beef should not be dull or gray. Choose lean cuts, but with a little bit of fat marbling for tenderness. Most of the beef recipes in this book call for lean, tender cuts such as tenderloin or sirloin, but you can also choose less expensive lean cuts such as flank, skirt, or top round.

If you buy beef or pork but won't be cooking it within its window of freshness, freeze it. It's fine to freeze meat in its original packaging for about a month, but if you need to store it for longer than that, double-wrap it in freezer bags so it doesn't get freezer burn.

Stock up on your favorite cuts, and store them in the freezer. They'll come in handy on those busy days when you don't have any meals planned, and will save you from emergency takeout dinners. As you prepare more dishes at home, you'll soon learn which types of meat you're cooking the most.

CUTTING AND PREPARING MEAT

Regardless of the type of meat or cut, always start with a sharp knife. Freeze the meat for about 30 minutes before cutting—this will make it a lot easier to slice and ensure clean, even cuts. Don't attempt to cut completely frozen meats—unless you have a kitchen saw designed for this use, it's futile, and probably a little dangerous.

THIN STRIPS: Trim any excess fat from the surface of the meat. Look for the direction of the grain. If the meat is more than about 2 inches wide, cut it along the grain into smaller strips. Then cut against the grain at a slight angle into thin, even slices about ¼ inch thick.

CUBES: Trim any excess fat from the surface of the meat. Slice long strips following the length of the meat, then dice those long strips into even, bite-size pieces.

MARINATING AND TENDERIZING

Velveting is a popular technique in Chinese cooking for chicken, pork, and beef, and it is what it sounds like—a trick to make the meat velvety tender. The meat is marinated in cornstarch and seasonings. The cornstarch acts as a barrier, protecting the meat from the wok's very high heat and helping seal in the moisture and juices of the meat as it cooks. This process results in very tender meat, especially when used with tenderloin or sirloin. Velveting is also important for less expensive cuts that might not be as tender, such as flank, skirt, or top sirloin.

It is safe to marinate meats at room temperature for about 30 minutes. If you need to marinate meat for a longer period, rub the seasonings and cornstarch on the meat first, then let it sit in the refrigerator. About 20 minutes before you are ready to stir-fry the meat, take it out of the refrigerator and leave it at room temperature.

STIR-FRYING MEAT

Your meat should be close to room temperature when you stir-fry. Meat straight from the refrigerator will cool down the wok's surface and prevent it from creating that nice sear. It may also cause the meat to stick to the wok.

Heat a wok over medium-high heat. As soon as it starts to smoke a little, add a bit of cooking oil. Use a wok spatula to spread the hot oil on the lower half of the wok's surface. Carefully drop the meat into the wok and use the spatula to spread the meat into a single layer. Wait about 20 to 30 seconds for the bottom of the meat to cook, then flip. Wait another 20 seconds then stir-fry the meat until it is fully cooked.

Note: If you use a less expensive steak such as flank, skirt, or top round, be sure to velvet it (see above, Marinating and Tenderizing), and take care not to overcook it or it can become tough.

STEAMED EGG WITH GROUND PORK

½ pound ground pork

2 teaspoons finely diced
Chinese preserved radish
(optional)

2 teaspoons soy sauce

1 teaspoon cornstarch

½ teaspoon salt

Pinch freshly ground
black pepper

3 eggs

½ cup water

1 teaspoon Shaoxing wine

SERVES 4 TO 6 AS PART OF A MULTICOURSE MEAL /
PREP TIME: 5 MINUTES, PLUS 15 MINUTES TO MARINATE /
COOK TIME: 15 MINUTES

Steamed Egg with Ground Pork is the paragon of Chinese
home cooking. It may look humble on the outside, but the
flavors it delivers are exquisite. There are so many different
versions that every family has their own recipe. However,
they all feature a soft and silky egg custard with a savory
ground pork mixture.

1. In a medium bowl, combine the ground pork, preserved
radish (if using), soy sauce, cornstarch, salt, and pepper,
mixing it well. Marinate at room temperature for about
15 minutes.

2. Set up a steaming rack in a wok, fill it with water halfway
up to the rack, and set the heat to medium.

3. In a separate bowl, whisk the eggs with the water and
Shaoxing wine. Set it aside.

4. Transfer the ground pork mixture to a shallow heatproof
dish. Spread the ground pork in a single layer to cover
the dish.

5. Pour the egg mixture evenly over the ground pork.

6. Cover the dish with aluminum foil. This will prevent water from dripping onto the custard.

7. When the water in the wok starts to boil, place the dish on the steaming rack.

8. Steam for about 15 minutes or until the custard is set, then serve.

Serving Tip

Serve with steamed white or brown rice (pages 20 and 22), or Congee (page 24).

Variation Tip

There are many possible additions to this dish. They include chopped scallions, diced shiitake or button mushrooms, ground chicken instead of pork, diced onion or shallots, diced 1,000 year-old-egg . . . the list goes on.

MOO SHU PORK LETTUCE WRAPS

1 head lettuce

FOR THE MARINADE

2 teaspoons soy sauce
2 teaspoons Shaoxing wine
2 teaspoons cornstarch
½ teaspoon salt
Pinch ground white pepper
1 pound pork tenderloin,
    cut into thin strips (like
    French fries)

FOR THE SAUCE

2 tablespoons hoisin sauce
1 tablespoon rice vinegar
1 tablespoon oyster sauce
1 teaspoon sugar
1 teaspoon soy sauce
½ teaspoon sesame oil

FOR THE STIR-FRY

2 tablespoons peanut oil
2-inch piece ginger, peeled
    and julienned
2 garlic cloves, minced
4 or 5 large shiitake
    mushrooms, thinly sliced
4 cups shredded cabbage
½ carrot, julienned
1 scallion, chopped
½ cup chopped fresh cilantro

SERVES 4 TO 6 AS PART OF A MULTICOURSE MEAL /
PREP TIME: 5 MINUTES, PLUS 20 MINUTES TO MARINATE /
COOK TIME: 5 MINUTES

Moo Shu Pork is traditionally served with thin pancakes, but this healthy spin makes use of lettuce wraps instead. Tender strips of pork tossed in a tangy sauce with cabbage and wrapped in chilled lettuce leaves—*ho chiak* (delicious)!

1. Separate and wash the lettuce leaves. Chill the leaves in the refrigerator until ready to serve.

2. Pour the soy sauce, Shaoxing wine, cornstarch, salt, and pepper over the pork and toss to combine and coat the meat. Marinate at room temperature for 20 minutes.

3. Meanwhile, in a small bowl, make the sauce by mixing together the hoisin sauce, rice vinegar, oyster sauce, sugar, soy sauce, and sesame oil. Set it aside.

4. In a wok over medium-high heat, heat the peanut oil.

5. Add the ginger and garlic and stir-fry until aromatic, or for about 20 seconds.

6. Add the pork and stir-fry for about 30 seconds.

7. Toss in the sliced shiitake mushrooms.

8. Once the pork and mushrooms are cooked all the way through, stir in the sauce and mix well.

9. Toss in the shredded cabbage and carrot, stir, and turn off the heat.

10. Transfer to a serving dish, garnish with the chopped scallion and cilantro, and serve with the chilled lettuce.

Cooking Tip

Packaged coleslaw mix with shredded cabbage and julienned carrots is a time-saver in the preparation of this dish!

PEKING-STYLE PORK RIBS

FOR THE MARINADE

2 teaspoons Chinese rose wine
2 pounds pork ribs, cut into
   about 1½-inch pieces
½ teaspoon salt
Pinch ground white pepper
¼ teaspoon five-spice powder
3 teaspoons cornstarch

FOR THE SAUCE

2 tablespoons ketchup
1½ tablespoons apple
   cider vinegar
2 teaspoons brown sugar
1 teaspoon soy sauce
½ teaspoon dark soy sauce
Pinch five-spice powder

FOR THE STIR-FRY

2 tablespoons peanut oil
2 garlic cloves, minced

SERVES 4 TO 6 AS PART OF A MULTICOURSE MEAL /
PREP TIME: 5 MINUTES, PLUS 20 MINUTES TO MARINATE /
COOK TIME: 5 MINUTES

There's no need to wait until summer to fire up your grill and enjoy some good pork ribs. These ribs are simple to make in a wok and ready in about 30 minutes. Great on their own, they also pair wonderfully with a bowl of steamed rice. And the sauce is out of this world!

1. Pour the Chinese rose wine over the pork. Add the salt, pepper, and five-spice powder. Mix well, then coat the pork with the cornstarch. Marinate at room temperature for 20 minutes.

2. In a small bowl, prepare the sauce by mixing together the ketchup, apple cider vinegar, brown sugar, soy sauce, dark soy sauce, and five-spice powder.

3. In a wok over medium-high heat, heat the peanut oil.

4. Arrange the pork ribs in the wok in a single layer. Cook without stirring for about 30 seconds, reduce the heat to medium, and stir-fry for about 5 minutes or until the pork is cooked and golden brown.

5. Add the garlic and stir-fry for about 20 seconds until aromatic.

6. Stir in the sauce, coating the ribs.

7. Transfer the ribs and sauce to a serving plate.

Variation Tip

Instead of pork ribs, you can also use thinly sliced pork tenderloin or pork shoulder. If you are using pork ribs, ask your butcher to cut them for you. Alternatively, you can grill whole pork ribs. If so, omit the cornstarch from the marinade and baste the sauce on the ribs 10 minutes before they are done.

Ingredient Tip

Chinese rose wine is a clear liquor made from sorghum. It is distilled with rose petals and rock sugar. You can buy it at any Asian supermarket or on Amazon.com.

PORK RIBS WITH BLACK BEAN SAUCE

FOR THE MARINADE

2 teaspoons Shaoxing wine
2 teaspoons cornstarch
½ teaspoon salt
Pinch ground white pepper
2 pounds pork ribs, cut into
    1½-inch pieces

FOR THE SAUCE

1½ cups water
2 tablespoons black
    bean sauce
2 teaspoons sugar
2 teaspoons soy sauce
1 teaspoon dark soy sauce

FOR THE STIR-FRY

2 tablespoons peanut oil
1-inch piece ginger, peeled
    and minced
2 garlic cloves, minced
1 scallion, chopped

SERVES 4 TO 6 AS PART OF A MULTICOURSE MEAL /
PREP TIME: 5 MINUTES, PLUS 20 MINUTES TO MARINATE /
COOK TIME: 25 MINUTES

Steamed pork ribs with black bean sauce is a popular dim sum dish. We're elevating the concept by stir-frying the ribs in a wok and letting them simmer in the tasty sauce. No need to wait until your next dim sum brunch to enjoy these pork ribs—make them at home for dinner tonight!

1. Pour the Shaoxing wine, cornstarch, salt, and pepper over the pork and toss to combine. Marinate at room temperature for about 20 minutes.

2. In a small bowl, prepare the sauce by mixing together the water, black bean sauce, sugar, soy sauce, and dark soy sauce. Set it aside.

3. In a wok over medium-high heat, heat the peanut oil.

4. Arrange the pork ribs in the wok in a single layer. Let them cook without stirring for 30 seconds, add the ginger and garlic, then flip the ribs with a wok spatula.

5. Cook, stirring every 10 seconds or so, for about 2 minutes.

6. Add the sauce, stir, and cover the wok.

7. Reduce the heat to low and simmer for about 20 minutes. Peek every few minutes to make sure the sauce is not evaporating too quickly. If it is, add water when necessary to keep it simmering until the last minute.

8. Transfer the ribs to a serving plate and garnish with the chopped scallion. Serve immediately.

Ingredient Tip

You can use preserved salted black beans in place of black bean sauce. They are whole beans instead of a paste, which gives the dish a slightly different flavor and texture.

Serving Tip

Enjoy this with steamed white or brown rice (pages 20 and 22).

SWEET AND SOUR PORK

FOR THE MARINADE

2 teaspoons Shaoxing wine
2 teaspoons cornstarch
½ teaspoon salt
Pinch ground white pepper
1 pound pork tenderloin or
  pork shoulder, cut into
  ¾-inch pieces

FOR THE STIR-FRY

2 tablespoons peanut oil
2 garlic cloves, minced
1 (8-ounce) can pineapple
  chunks, drained
1 small onion, cut into wedges
1 green or yellow bell pepper,
  cut into 1-inch pieces
¼ cup Sweet and Sour Sauce
  (page 27)
1 scallion, cut into
  1-inch pieces

**SERVES 4 TO 6 AS PART OF A MULTICOURSE MEAL /
PREP TIME: 5 MINUTES, PLUS 20 MINUTES TO MARINATE /
COOK TIME: 10 MINUTES**

Sweet and sour pork is one of my all-time favorite dishes.
This is a healthier version of the popular dish with stir-fried
pork smothered in a delectable sauce alongside pineapple
chunks, onion, and bell pepper. It's paradise on a plate. Let
it transport you—with steamed rice of course!

1. Pour the Shaoxing wine, cornstarch, salt, and pepper over
the pork and toss to combine. Marinate at room temperature
for about 20 minutes.

2. In a wok over medium-high heat, heat the peanut oil.

3. Add the pork in batches to the wok in a single layer.
Allow the bottom of the pork to cook through before flipping. Stir-fry until fully cooked, then remove the pork from
the wok and set it aside.

4. Stir-fry the garlic for about 20 seconds until aromatic,
adding a touch more oil if necessary.

5. Add the pineapple chunks, onion, and bell pepper to the wok. Stir-fry until the onions are slightly translucent.

6. Stir in the sweet and sour sauce, mixing well to combine.

7. Return the cooked pork to the wok along with the scallion. Stir to combine all the ingredients.

8. Transfer to a serving dish and serve immediately.

Variation Tip

If you absolutely must have the crispy batter on the pork, oven-bake the pork pieces instead of deep-frying them. Dip each piece of marinated pork in egg, dredge it with panko breadcrumbs, and spread them on a lightly oiled baking sheet. Bake at 375°F for 20 minutes, or until they turn a nice golden brown, then toss them in the wok with the vegetables just to coat them in the sauce. Double the amount of sweet and sour sauce as the panko breadcrumbs will absorb a good amount.

PORK AND MIXED VEGETABLE STIR-FRY

FOR THE MARINADE

2 teaspoons cornstarch
½ teaspoon salt
Pinch ground white pepper
½ pound boneless pork chop,
    cut into thin strips

FOR THE STIR-FRY

2 tablespoons peanut oil
1-inch piece ginger, peeled
    and julienned
2 garlic cloves, minced
1 small head broccoli,
    cut into florets
1 tablespoon water
1 red bell pepper, sliced
1 cup snow peas
1 small onion, cut into wedges
2 to 3 tablespoons All Purpose
    Stir-Fry Sauce (page 26)
½ teaspoon toasted
    sesame seeds

SERVES 4 TO 6 AS PART OF A MULTICOURSE MEAL /
PREP TIME: 5 MINUTES, PLUS 20 MINUTES TO MARINATE /
COOK TIME: 5 MINUTES

Like the Mixed Vegetable Stir Fry (page 59), this is a versatile dish for just about any vegetable, and a great way to use up those leftover veggies in the refrigerator. Try string beans, carrots, baby corn, bamboo shoots, sugar snap peas, mushrooms, and bok choy. Choose no more than four vegetables to keep the dish simple.

1. Sprinkle the cornstarch, salt, and pepper evenly over the pork and mix to combine. Marinate at room temperature for 20 minutes.

2. In a wok over medium-high heat, heat the peanut oil.

3. Add the pork and stir-fry until fully cooked. Remove the pork from the wok and set it aside.

4. Add the ginger and garlic to the wok and stir-fry for about 20 seconds, until aromatic.

5. Add the broccoli florets, stir-fry for a few seconds, and add the water to help steam the broccoli.

6. Add the bell pepper, snow peas, and onion, and stir-fry until the onion turns slightly translucent.

7. Return the pork to the wok and add the stir-fry sauce. Toss for a few seconds to combine all the ingredients, then transfer the dish to a serving plate.

8. Sprinkle the sesame seeds on top just before serving.

FIVE-SPICE PORK

FOR THE MARINADE

2 teaspoons Shaoxing wine

2 teaspoons cornstarch

½ teaspoon Chinese
five-spice powder

½ teaspoon salt

Pinch ground white pepper

1 pound pork tenderloin or
shoulder, cut into thin strips

FOR THE SAUCE

1 tablespoon soy sauce

2 teaspoons honey

½ teaspoon brown sugar

½ teaspoon dark soy sauce

½ teaspoon Chinese
five-spice powder

FOR THE STIR-FRY

2 tablespoons peanut oil

2 garlic cloves, minced

SERVES 4 TO 6 AS PART OF A MULTICOURSE MEAL /
PREP TIME: 5 MINUTES, PLUS 20 MINUTES TO MARINATE /
COOK TIME: 5 MINUTES

Like Chinese Pork Meatballs (page 38), this is another spin-off from the popular Chinatown favorite, *char siew*, or Cantonese-style barbecue pork. But instead of marinating the pork for hours and then grilling or broiling it, this recipe stir-fries it in a wok, then smothers it in a sweet sauce flavored with Chinese five-spice. Pair with steamed white or brown rice (pages 20 and 22) to soak up the saucy goodness.

1. Pour the Shaoxing wine, cornstarch, five-spice powder, salt, and pepper over the pork and toss to combine. Marinate at room temperature for 20 minutes.

2. In a small bowl, prepare the sauce by combining the soy sauce, honey, brown sugar, dark soy sauce, and five-spice powder.

3. In a wok over medium-high heat, heat the peanut oil.

4. Add the pork and stir-fry until slightly golden brown.

5. Add the garlic and stir-fry for about 20 seconds.

6. Stir in the sauce, tossing well to coat the pork, and transfer to a serving dish. Serve immediately.

SICHUAN TWICE-COOKED PORK

1 pound pork shoulder
Water for boiling
   pork shoulder

FOR THE SAUCE

1 tablespoon black bean paste
1 tablespoon soy sauce
1 teaspoon chili bean paste
½ teaspoon sugar
Pinch salt

FOR THE STIR-FRY

1 tablespoon peanut oil
2 garlic cloves, minced
1 leek, cut into 1-inch pieces
1 green bell pepper, cut into
   bite-size pieces

SERVES 4 AS PART OF A MULTICOURSE MEAL /
PREP TIME: 25 MINUTES / COOK TIME: 5 MINUTES

This spicy dish is traditionally made with paper-thin sliced pork belly, but this recipe uses pork shoulder as a healthier alternative. Its name is derived from the double cooking method in which the pork is first boiled, then stir-fried. Boiling the meat firms it up so you can cut it into those super-thin slices, and also prepares it for stir-frying.

1. Fill a medium pot with enough water to cover the pork shoulder. Bring the water to a boil over high heat and lower the pork into the pot.

2. Reduce the heat to medium, cover, and simmer for 20 minutes.

3. Remove the pork from the water and let it cool. Keep it in the refrigerator until you are ready to cook the dish.

4. In a small bowl, prepare the sauce by mixing together the black bean paste, soy sauce, chili bean paste, sugar, and salt.

5. When the meat has cooled and you are ready to prepare the dish, slice it into the thinnest pieces possible with a very sharp knife.

6. In a wok over medium-high heat, heat the peanut oil.

7. Add the pork and stir-fry the slices until they turn slightly brown around the edges. Remove the pork from the wok and set it aside.

8. Add more oil to the wok if needed, add the garlic, and stir-fry for about 20 seconds, until aromatic.

9. Add the leek and bell pepper, stir-fry for about 1 minute, and return the pork to the wok.

10. Add the black bean sauce, stir well, and transfer the dish to a serving plate.

Substitution Tip

Instead of leeks, you can use scallions cut into 1-inch pieces.

BEEF AND BELL PEPPER STIR-FRY

SERVES 4 TO 6 AS PART OF A MULTICOURSE MEAL /
PREP TIME: 5 MINUTES, PLUS 20 MINUTES TO MARINATE /
COOK TIME: 5 MINUTES

FOR THE MARINADE

2 teaspoons cornstarch
½ teaspoon salt
½ teaspoon ground
   black pepper
1 pound flank steak,
   thinly sliced

FOR THE SAUCE

1 tablespoon soy sauce
1 teaspoon black bean sauce
½ teaspoon dark soy sauce
½ teaspoon sugar
½ teaspoon sesame oil

FOR THE STIR-FRY

2 tablespoons peanut oil
2 cloves garlic, minced
1 red bell pepper, cut into
   thin strips
1 green bell pepper,
   cut into thin strips
1 fresh red or green chile,
   cut into strips (optional)
1 onion, cut into rings

There is something magical about the beef, bell pepper, and onion combination. It reminds me of a Mexican steak fajita with a Chinese twist that includes black bean sauce. You can add thin strips of fresh chile if you like it spicy, and by all means, serve this over warm steamed white or brown rice (pages 20 and 22).

1. Sprinkle the cornstarch, salt, and pepper over the beef, and toss to combine. Marinate at room temperature for about 20 minutes.

2. In a small bowl, prepare the sauce by mixing together the soy sauce, black bean sauce, dark soy sauce, sugar, and sesame oil. Set it aside.

3. In a wok over high heat, heat the peanut oil.

4. Arrange the beef in the wok in a single layer. Cook without stirring for about 20 seconds, flip the beef, and continue to stir-fry until fully cooked, about 1 minute.

5. Remove the beef from the wok.

6. Add a little more oil to the wok if needed, then add the garlic, red and green bell peppers, chile (if using), and onion. Avoid stirring too much, just toss lightly so the high heat can blister the peppers.

7. Return the beef to the wok and add the sauce. Stir to combine all the ingredients and transfer to a serving dish.

Ingredient Tip

When choosing bell peppers at the grocery store, check them on the bottom. Bell peppers have either three or four points. Peppers with three points are less sweet, which makes them a better choice for stir-frying. Peppers with four points are a little sweeter and are best eaten raw.

MONGOLIAN BEEF

FOR THE MARINADE

2 teaspoons cornstarch
½ teaspoon salt
Pinch freshly ground
    black pepper
1 pound flank steak or sirloin
    steak, thinly sliced

FOR THE SAUCE

1 tablespoon soy sauce
1 tablespoon water
1 teaspoon brown sugar
1 teaspoon rice vinegar

FOR THE STIR-FRY

2 tablespoons peanut oil
1-inch piece ginger, peeled
    and julienned
2 garlic cloves, minced
1 scallion, cut into
    1-inch pieces

SERVES 4 AS PART OF A MULTICOURSE MEAL /
PREP TIME: 5 MINUTES, PLUS 20 MINUTES TO MARINATE /
COOK TIME: 5 MINUTES

Despite the name, Mongolian Beef is actually a Chinese-American classic. Every restaurant has their own version, but it is essentially thin strips of tender beef in a sweet and tangy soy sauce, garnished with scallions. It sounds simple but it is ridiculously good and so easy to make. Serve with white or brown steamed rice (pages 20 and 22).

1. Sprinkle the cornstarch, salt, and pepper over the beef and toss to combine. Marinate at room temperature for 20 minutes.

2. In a small bowl, prepare the sauce by mixing together the soy sauce, water, brown sugar, and rice vinegar.

3. In a wok over medium-high heat, heat the peanut oil.

4. Add the beef and fry just until the surfaces turn brown.

5. Add the ginger and garlic, and stir-fry until fragrant, 2 or 3 seconds.

6. Add the sauce and stir to coat the beef.

7. Turn off the heat and add the scallion. Give it one last stir to very lightly heat up the scallions but not to cook them.

8. Transfer the dish to a serving plate.

Cooking Tip

If you like your Mongolian beef spicy, add a pinch of red pepper flakes to the sauce. You can also add a few dried red chiles when stir-frying the beef.

BEEF WITH HONEY AND BLACK PEPPER SAUCE

FOR THE MARINADE

3 teaspoons cornstarch
½ teaspoon salt
¼ teaspoon black pepper
1 pound beef tenderloin or
    steak, cut into thin slices

FOR THE SAUCE

3 tablespoons honey
2½ tablespoons low-sodium
    soy sauce
2 tablespoons water
2 teaspoons oyster sauce
1 teaspoon freshly ground
    black pepper

FOR THE STIR-FRY

2 tablespoons peanut oil
½ onion, thinly sliced
2 garlic cloves, minced

SERVES 4 TO 6 AS PART OF A MULTICOURSE MEAL /
PREP TIME: 5 MINUTES, PLUS 15 MINUTES TO MARINATE /
COOK TIME: 5 MINUTES

Even though this dish is so simple to make that you can have it on your dinner table in under 30 minutes, it tastes like it came from the best Chinese restaurant in town. The bold black pepper sauce is delectable and has a kick, so decrease the black pepper if you don't like it too spicy.

1. Sprinkle the cornstarch, salt, and pepper over the beef and toss to combine. Marinate at room temperature for 15 minutes.

2. In a small bowl, prepare the sauce by mixing together the honey, soy sauce, water, oyster sauce, and pepper.

3. In a wok over medium-high heat, heat the peanut oil.

4. Add the beef and stir-fry until just browned, remove from the wok, and set it aside.

5. Toss the onion and garlic into the wok and stir-fry until the onion turns slightly translucent.

6. Return the beef to the wok and add the sauce, stirring to coat the beef.

7. Turn off the heat and transfer to a serving plate.

BEEF WITH BROCCOLI

FOR THE MARINADE

2 teaspoons cornstarch

1 teaspoon soy sauce

Pinch freshly ground
    black pepper

½ pound tenderloin or sirloin
    steak, thinly sliced

FOR THE STIR-FRY

1½ tablespoons peanut oil

3 garlic cloves, minced

2 heads broccoli,
    cut into florets

¼ cup water

½ cup Brown Sauce (page 28)

SERVES 6 AS PART OF A MULTICOURSE MEAL /
PREP TIME: 5 MINUTES, PLUS 20 MINUTES TO MARINATE /
COOK TIME: 5 MINUTES

This is a Chinese takeout favorite that can be made even more delicious at home and at a fraction of the cost. Tender strips of beef are paired with broccoli and coated with a rich brown sauce.

1. Pour the cornstarch, soy sauce, and pepper over the beef and toss to combine. Marinate at room temperature for 20 minutes.

2. In a wok over medium-high heat, heat the peanut oil.

3. Add the beef and stir-fry just until no longer pink. Remove the beef from the wok and set it aside.

4. Add the garlic and stir-fry for 2 or 3 seconds. Add the broccoli florets and water to help steam the broccoli.

5. When the water has evaporated, return the beef to the wok.

6. Add the brown sauce and give everything a good stir.

7. As soon as the sauce thickens, turn off the heat and transfer the dish to a serving plate.

Ingredient Tip

Instead of stir-frying the broccoli, you can steam it in the wok or microwave ahead of time, then toss it in the wok with the beef to coat it in the sauce just before serving.

Better Than Takeout

A 5.4-ounce serving of Broccoli Beef at Panda Express has 520 milligrams of sodium. In this recipe, the same serving contains only 157 milligrams of sodium.

SICHUAN BEEF

FOR THE MARINADE

2 teaspoons cornstarch

1 teaspoon sesame oil

1 teaspoon soy sauce

1 pound beef tenderloin or
sirloin, cut into ¼-inch strips
(like French fries)

FOR THE SAUCE

1 tablespoon soy sauce

1 teaspoon brown sugar

1 teaspoon sesame oil

1 teaspoon chili oil

½ tablespoon oyster sauce

¼ teaspoon dark soy sauce

FOR THE STIR-FRY

2 tablespoons peanut oil

2 garlic cloves, minced

5 or 6 dried red chiles

½ carrot, julienned

1 scallion, chopped

SERVES 4 AS PART OF A MULTICOURSE MEAL /
PREP TIME: 5 MINUTES, PLUS 15 MINUTES TO MARINATE /
COOK TIME: 5 MINUTES

This weeknight-friendly stir-fry features shreds of beef in a
sweet and spicy sauce. The julienned carrots provide a little
extra sweetness and crunch. Sichuan cuisine is celebrated
for its spicy dishes, but you control how much chile to add
to this one.

1. Pour the cornstarch, sesame oil, and soy sauce over the
beef and toss to combine. Marinate at room temperature
for 15 minutes.

2. In a small bowl, prepare the sauce by mixing together
the soy sauce, brown sugar, sesame oil, chili oil, oyster
sauce, and dark soy sauce. Set it aside.

3. In a wok over medium-high heat, heat the peanut oil.

4. Add the beef and stir-fry for about 30 seconds.

5. Add the garlic and stir-fry until the beef is almost cooked.

6. Add the sauce and dried red chiles, tossing to combine all the ingredients.

7. Turn off the heat, add the carrot, and give the dish one last stir.

8. Transfer the beef to a serving plate and garnish with the chopped scallion.

Substitution Tip

Instead of chili oil, you can use Sichuan peppercorns, Sriracha sauce, chili garlic sauce, or red pepper flakes. If using red pepper flakes, use only ½ teaspoon unless you like to venture into fiery territory!

BEEF WITH SHIITAKE MUSHROOMS

2 cups whole dried shiitake
   mushrooms
5 cups boiling water

FOR THE MARINADE

2 teaspoons soy sauce
2 teaspoons cornstarch
Pinch freshly ground
   black pepper
1 pound beef tenderloin or
   sirloin, cut into thin strips

FOR THE SAUCE

2 tablespoons oyster sauce
1 tablespoon soy sauce
2 teaspoons brown sugar
½ teaspoon sesame oil

FOR THE STIR-FRY

2 tablespoons peanut oil
1 scallion, chopped

SERVES 4 TO 6 AS PART OF A MULTICOURSE MEAL /
PREP TIME: 5 MINUTES, PLUS 20 MINUTES TO MARINATE /
COOK TIME 5 MINUTES

This quick stir-fry combines shiitake mushrooms with tender beef in a sweet oyster sauce. Dried shiitake mushrooms are better than fresh mushrooms in this dish since they have a deeper flavor. Serve with steamed white or brown rice (pages 20 and 22) so it can soak up the luscious sauce.

1. Soak the dried shiitake mushrooms in boiling water for about 20 minutes.

2. Meanwhile, pour the soy sauce, cornstarch, and pepper over the beef, and toss to combine. Marinate at room temperature for about 20 minutes.

3. In a small bowl, make the sauce by mixing together the oyster sauce, soy sauce, brown sugar, and sesame oil. Set it aside.

4. Drain and discard the water from the mushrooms, cut off and discard the mushroom stems, and gently squeeze the caps to remove excess water.

5. Cut the mushrooms into thin slices.

6. In a wok over medium-high heat, heat the peanut oil.

7. Add the beef and stir-fry for about 30 seconds, then remove it from the wok.

8. Add the sliced mushrooms, along with a little more peanut oil if needed. Stir-fry for about 2 minutes, then stir in the sauce.

9. Return the beef to the wok, toss to combine all the ingredients, and transfer to a serving dish.

10. Garnish with the chopped scallion and serve immediately.

Cooking Tip

If you have time, instead of boiling them, you can soak the dried shiitake mushrooms for a few hours at room temperature to soften them.

Kung Pao Shrimp, page 135

Seafood

Cooking with Seafood

Seafood is a big seller in Chinese cuisine. It's not uncommon to see large fish tanks in Chinese restaurants housing live fish, lobsters, and crabs that customers can pick out to be cooked for their dinner. It doesn't get any fresher than that!

In the United States, shrimp is the most popular seafood—it's certainly one of my family's favorites. With an endless variety of Chinese flavor combinations for shrimp, you'll have many heavenly meals, most of which take just a few minutes to put together.

BUYING FISH

Fish is a popular protein, as it tends to have a mild flavor that goes with a wide variety of sauces. Fish is also lean, making it a healthy choice. Since it flakes easily, most fish don't stir-fry very well unless deep-fried in a light batter first. Either steaming or pan-frying usually works best for cooking fish.

If choosing a whole fish—common in Chinese cuisine—take a look at the eyes. They should be clear, wet, and bright. They should not look cloudy or dull. Pry open the side to expose the gills, which should be a very bright red color. If you are buying a fish fillet, gently press on the surface. It should feel firm and spring back without leaving an indentation.

Fish can be refrigerated for only about 2 days, so it's best to either cook it as quickly as possible or freeze it.

BUYING SHRIMP

Depending on where you live, shrimp might be one of the few foods that are better bought frozen than fresh, since most are frozen very quickly right at the source. A lot of the fresh shrimp at supermarkets were previously frozen, then thawed.

Shrimp packaging usually lists the number of shrimp needed to make 1 pound. For example, if you see 31/35 on the package, it means that it takes 31 to 35 of that size of shrimp to make 1 pound. For most recipes, I like to use large shrimp (31/35) or extra large (26/30). Avoid precooked shrimp unless you are using them for cold salads, otherwise they'll end up being overcooked. Also, buy them with the shell on. These tend to be less expensive and they taste fresher when cooked.

Let shrimp thaw in the refrigerator overnight, or if you are in a hurry, place the shrimp in a bowl and set it in the kitchen sink under a very slow stream of cool water. The shrimp should be fully thawed in about 15 minutes.

HOW TO PEEL AND DEVEIN SHRIMP

Keep the shrimp on ice as your peel and devein them—this keeps them cold and fresh.

If the head is still on, remove it by gently twisting it. Next, starting near the legs of the shrimp, peel the shell off. If you would like to keep the tail on for aesthetics, simply leave the tail intact and remove the rest of the shell. If you want the tail gone, gently pressing on the meaty part of the tail with your thumb and your forefinger can also release the flesh from the shell. This makes it easier to peel the rest of the shrimp.

To devein the shrimp, use a small paring knife to make a shallow incision along the top of the shrimp's back. Use the tip of the knife to assist with removing the black vein. I like to have a small stream of running tap water when I devein shrimp so I can rinse them off easily as I clean them.

HOW TO COOK AND CUT CRABS

Bring a large pot of salted water to a boil (the water should be salty like the ocean). Lower the crabs into the boiling water, and cover the pot. They take about 10 minutes per pound to cook, and turn red or orange when fully cooked. Remove the crabs from the water and let them cool. Sit them in ice to speed the cooling process.

To cut the crab, start by peeling off the top shell. Remove the gills and the mouth parts. Next, flip the crab over and pull off the apron in the middle of the body (the apron is shaped like a thin upside-down triangle). You should now be able to snap the crab into two halves right down the middle. Rinse away any yellowish-green residue. Finally, peel the claws from the body.

HOW TO CLEAN CLAMS

Always buy clams the day you will cook them, as they don't stay fresh for long. Before you begin cleaning the clams, inspect them to make sure there are no broken clams, which are most likely dead or unhealthy. Discard any clams that are wide open. If you see a clam that is partially open, gently tap on it—if it closes, it's still alive, but if it remains open, it is likely dead and should be discarded.

Give the clams a good rinse then put them in a large bowl of salted water at room temperature. All of the clams should be submerged in the water. After a while, they will start to spit out water. Some of the clams on the top can spit quite far so keep them covered with a damp towel to avoid getting your kitchen countertop wet! As they spit out water, they will also naturally clean out their insides of any dirt and mud. You can keep them submerged in the salted water for a few hours until ready to cook.

STIR-FRYING SEAFOOD

As mentioned earlier, fish is not a good candidate for stir-frying because it tends to flake. If used in a stir-fry dish, it usually must first be dipped in batter and deep-fried, which is not a very healthy option. The healthiest way to cook fish in a wok is to either steam or pan-fry it in a very light coating of oil, just so the fish doesn't stick to the wok's surface.

Shrimp and squid are great options for stir-frying because they are firm and can withstand the constant tossing. They both take very little time to cook, so watch carefully in order to not overcook them. Shrimp curl into a "C" shape and are opaque and slightly firm when cooked. When cooking squid, it helps to first blanch them for a few seconds to prep them for the stir-fry.

Also, shrimp can be stir-fried with the shell on, but only in certain recipes. You won't be able to char the shrimp meat, but you can char the shell just slightly without overcooking the shrimp, which gives it a nice toasty flavor. It's a bit more tedious to remove the shell while at the dinner table, but for a shrimp lover who wants to try it in every way, this method does give the shrimp a different texture and flavor.

PAN-FRIED FISH WITH SOY SAUCE

FOR THE PAN-FRIED FISH

1½ pounds white fish fillet
(cod, tilapia, or red snapper),
cut into two or three pieces
Salt
Pepper
1 to 2 tablespoons cornstarch
1½ tablespoons peanut oil
2 tablespoons chopped
scallions (optional)

FOR THE SAUCE

1 tablespoon soy sauce
½ teaspoon sesame oil
½ teaspoon sugar

SERVES 4 AS PART OF A MULTICOURSE MEAL /
PREP TIME: 5 MINUTES / COOK TIME: 5 MINUTES

Pan-fried fish is one of my favorite dishes cooked by my mom. Slightly crunchy on the outside with just a hint of soy sauce, but soft and flaky on the inside, it sounds simple but is so memorably good. This family dish is shared as part of a multicourse meal, and pairs well with steamed rice.

1. Pat the fish dry with a paper towel. Season on both sides with salt and pepper, and dust with the cornstarch.

2. In a wok over medium-high heat, heat the peanut oil.

3. When the wok is smoking very slightly, place the fillets in the wok and leave untouched for about 3 minutes.

4. While the fish is cooking, make the sauce by whisking together the soy sauce, sesame oil, and sugar. Set it aside.

5. Gently flip the fish to cook on the other side for about 1 minute.

6. Test the fish with a fork. If it flakes easily, it is cooked.

7. Turn off the heat and pour the sauce into the wok around around the fish. Flip the fish one more time to coat and transfer it to a serving plate.

8. Garnish with the chopped scallions (if using), and serve immediately.

CLASSIC CHINESE STEAMED FISH FILLET

FOR THE SAUCE

2 tablespoons soy sauce

1 tablespoon water

2 teaspoons Shaoxing wine

1 teaspoon sesame oil

½ teaspoon sugar

Pinch ground white pepper

FOR THE STEAMED FISH

1 teaspoon sesame oil

1½ pounds white fish fillet
(such as cod or red snapper)

½ teaspoon salt

2 pinches ground white pepper

2-inch piece ginger, peeled,
half sliced and half julienned

1 tablespoon peanut oil

2 scallions, julienned

¼ cup fresh cilantro leaves

SERVES 4 AS PART OF A MULTICOURSE MEAL /
PREP TIME: 10 MINUTES / COOK TIME 7 MINUTES

While steamed fish is a popular Chinese dish often served at weddings and birthday celebrations, it can also be regularly found on home dinner tables. Traditionally, the whole fish is served, including the tail and the head. Some people are not big fans of this presentation, so here is a quick, simple, and practical way to enjoy Chinese Steamed Fish using fish fillets.

1. In a small bowl, make the sauce by combining the soy sauce, water, Shaoxing wine, sesame oil, sugar, and pepper. Set it aside.

2. Set up a metal steaming rack in a wok and pour water into the wok halfway up to the bottom of the steaming plate. Turn the heat to medium-high.

3. Rub the sesame oil over the entire surface of the fish fillet and season both sides with salt and pepper.

4. Place the fish fillet on a heatproof dish and arrange the sliced ginger on top of the fish.

5. Cover and steam for 5 minutes or until the fish is cooked (it should flake easily with a fork).

6. Transfer the fish to a serving plate, discarding the ginger slices.

7. Discard the water from the wok, return the wok to the burner, and dry over medium heat.

8. Once the wok has completely dried, add the peanut oil to the wok followed by the julienned ginger. When the ginger starts to turn golden brown, add the sauce. Allow the sauce to boil for just a few seconds, then use a wok spatula or ladle to spoon the sauce over the fish.

9. Garnish with the scallions and cilantro leaves, and serve immediately.

Ingredient Tip

Place the julienned scallions into a small bowl of ice-cold water to make them curl up. This makes a very pretty garnish.

CRAB EGG FOO YOUNG

FOR THE SAUCE

1 cup Basic Chinese Chicken
Stock (page 25), or
store bought
1 tablespoon oyster sauce
2 teaspoons soy sauce
2 teaspoons cornstarch
½ teaspoon sesame oil

FOR THE MARINADE

4 eggs
1 teaspoon soy sauce
½ teaspoon salt
Pinch ground white pepper

FOR THE EGG FOO YOUNG

4 tablespoons peanut
oil, divided
½ small yellow onion, diced
2 cups fresh bean sprouts
1 tablespoon water
1 cup cooked crabmeat
½ cup chopped scallion

SERVES 4 TO 6 AS PART OF A MULTICOURSE MEAL /
PREP TIME: 10 MINUTES / COOK TIME: 20 MINUTES

This hearty Chinese-style omelet with crabmeat, bean
sprouts, and chopped scallion is smothered in a rich brown
sauce. There's no need to wait for dinner; skip the brown
sauce and enjoy these omelets for breakfast!

1. In a small bowl, prepare the sauce by combining the
chicken stock, oyster sauce, soy sauce, cornstarch, and
sesame oil. Set it aside.

2. In a separate bowl, season the eggs with the soy sauce,
salt, and pepper. Beat lightly until well combined.

3. In a wok over medium heat, heat 1 tablespoon of
peanut oil.

4. Add the onion and stir-fry until translucent.

5. Add the fresh bean sprouts and water to the wok, and
stir-fry for about 20 seconds.

6. When all the water has evaporated and the bean sprouts have softened a little, add the crabmeat and scallions. Turn off the heat and transfer the crab mixture to a large bowl.

7. Pour the eggs over the crab mixture and stir to combine.

8. Place the wok over medium-high heat, and add the remaining 3 tablespoons of peanut oil.

9. Pour about ⅓ cup of the egg-crab mixture into the wok. Cook until golden brown, or for about 2 minutes on each side. Set it aside. Repeat the process with the remaining mixture, ⅓ cup at a time.

10. Stir the sauce well and pour it into the wok. Simmer until the sauce thickens, then spoon the sauce over the egg foo young patties.

Variation Tip

Try this dish with shrimp instead of crab.

GINGER AND SCALLION CRAB

FOR THE SAUCE

4 tablespoons water

1½ tablespoons oyster sauce

1 teaspoon soy sauce

½ teaspoon sesame oil

½ teaspoon sugar

½ teaspoon cornstarch

Pinch ground white pepper

FOR THE STIR-FRY

1 tablespoon peanut oil

2-inch piece ginger, peeled
and sliced

4 whole Dungeness or blue
crabs (about 2 pounds each),
cooked, cleaned, and cut
(see page 123)

2 scallions, cut into
1-inch pieces

**SERVES 4 TO 6 AS PART OF A MULTICOURSE MEAL /
PREP TIME: 10 MINUTES / COOK TIME: 5 MINUTES**

Ginger and scallion is a classic Chinese flavor combination, and in this recipe, the unique taste really shines through. If you prefer, you can toss whole cooked crabs into your wok and stir-fry them in the yummy sauce. No need for forks, spoons, or chopsticks, but may I suggest having lots of napkins handy?

1. In a small bowl, make the sauce by mixing together the water, oyster sauce, soy sauce, sesame oil, sugar, corn-starch, and pepper.

2. Pour the peanut oil into the wok along with the ginger slices. Turn the heat to medium-high. Stir-fry the ginger until it is aromatic.

3. Add the crab and the sauce to the wok. Toss to coat the crab in the sauce.

4. Once the sauce thickens, turn off the heat and add the scallions. Stir-fry for a few seconds.

5. Transfer to a serving dish and serve immediately.

Cooking Tip

The fresher the crabs, the better. If you're not comfortable working with live crabs, you can find precooked crabs in most grocery stores. If you don't mind cooking live crabs, awesome!

ASIAN STIR-FRIED CLAMS

FOR THE SAUCE

¼ cup water

1 tablespoon oyster sauce

2 teaspoons soy sauce

½ teaspoon Shaoxing wine

½ teaspoon brown sugar

¼ teaspoon chicken stock granules (see page 6)

FOR THE STIR-FRY

1 teaspoon cornstarch

2 tablespoons water

2 tablespoons peanut oil

2 stalks lemongrass, white portion only, halved

½-inch piece ginger, peeled and thinly sliced

2 garlic cloves, minced

1½ pounds fresh clams

1 fresh red chile, thinly sliced

1 scallion, cut into 1-inch pieces

SERVES 4 AS PART OF A MULTICOURSE MEAL /
PREP TIME: 5 MINUTES / COOK TIME: 15 MINUTES

This tasty dish features fresh clams stir-fried with classic Chinese seasoning and a hint of lemongrass, a combination that creates a luscious sauce. It can be served as an appetizer or as a main dish over steamed rice.

1. In a small bowl, make the sauce by mixing together the water, oyster sauce, soy sauce, Shaoxing wine, brown sugar, and chicken stock granules. Set it aside.

2. In a separate small bowl, mix together the cornstarch and water. Set it aside.

3. In a wok over medium-high heat, heat the peanut oil.

4. Add the lemongrass and stir-fry for 1 to 2 minutes, or until the edges start to brown a little.

5. Add the ginger and garlic and stir-fry for about 20 seconds until it's aromatic.

6. Add the clams, and give all the ingredients a good stir.

7. Stir in the sauce and let it simmer.

8. When the clams start to open up, stir in the cornstarch mixture. Cover the wok if desired. By the time the sauce thickens, 20 to 30 seconds, most if not all of the clams should be open. Discard any unopened clams.

9. Turn off the heat, and transfer the clams to a serving plate. Garnish with the red chile and scallion.

Variation Tip

Try this recipe with fresh mussels instead of clams.

SCALLOPS WITH SNOW PEAS

SERVES 4 TO 6 AS PART OF A MULTICOURSE MEAL /
PREP TIME: 10 MINUTES / COOK TIME: 10 MINUTES

Scallops are the perfect match for the snow peas in this dish. Here's a luscious, healthy, weeknight meal—you can have it on your dinner table in under 30 minutes. Enjoy over steamed white or brown rice (pages 20 and 22), or steamed quinoa (page 23).

FOR THE SAUCE

2 tablespoons water

1 tablespoon oyster sauce

1 teaspoon soy sauce

½ teaspoon sugar

½ teaspoon sesame oil

FOR THE STIR-FRY

1 tablespoon water

1 teaspoon cornstarch

1 pound fresh bay scallops

½ teaspoon salt

Pinch ground white pepper

Pinch sugar

2½ tablespoons peanut
   oil, divided

2-inch piece ginger, peeled
   and minced

2 garlic cloves, minced

¾ pound snow peas, trimmed
   and strings removed.

1. In a small bowl, prepare the sauce by combining the water, oyster sauce, soy sauce, sugar, and sesame oil. Set it aside.

2. In a separate small bowl, mix together the water and cornstarch. Set it aside.

3. Rinse the scallops and pat them dry with paper towel. Season them with the salt, pepper, and pinch of sugar.

4. In a wok over medium-high heat, heat 1½ tablespoons of peanut oil.

5. Add the scallops and stir-fry for about 4 minutes. Remove the scallops and set them aside.

6. Add the remaining 1 tablespoon of peanut oil to the wok. Add the ginger and garlic and stir-fry until aromatic, or for about 30 seconds.

7. Add the snow peas and stir-fry until bright green, for about 1 minute. Stir in the sauce.

8. Once the snow peas have softened, add the cornstarch mixture. Stir-fry until the sauce begins to thicken.

9. Return the scallops to the wok and after a very quick stir-fry, transfer the dish to a serving plate.

Ingredient Tip

Instead of bay scallops, you can also use large diver scallops. Rather than stir-frying diver scallops, sear them for about
2 minutes on each side.

MUSSELS IN BLACK BEAN SAUCE

FOR THE SAUCE

1 cup water
1 tablespoon black bean sauce
1 teaspoon rice vinegar
1 teaspoon sugar
1 teaspoon soy sauce
½ teaspoon dark soy sauce

FOR THE STIR-FRY

1 tablespoon peanut oil
2-inch piece ginger, peeled
    and julienned
2 garlic cloves, minced
2 pounds fresh mussels,
    scrubbed and debearded
1 teaspoon sesame oil
1 scallion, chopped into
    1-inch pieces

SERVES 4 TO 6 AS PART OF A MULTICOURSE MEAL /
PREP TIME: 5 MINUTES / COOK TIME: 5 MINUTES

Mussels are great seafood on their own, but pair them with black bean sauce and you get a special briny sauce. They can be served as an appetizer or as part of a multicourse meal over steamed rice. You will love how incredibly easy this recipe is—and budget-friendly to boot.

1. In a small bowl, prepare the sauce by combining the water, black bean sauce, rice vinegar, sugar, soy sauce, and dark soy sauce. Set it aside.

2. In a wok over medium-high heat, heat the peanut oil.

3. Add the ginger and garlic and stir-fry for about 20 seconds or until aromatic.

4. Add the mussels and sauce. Stir and reduce the heat to low.

5. Cover the wok for about 5 minutes, uncovering to stir the contents every minute or so.

6. When most of the shells have opened, turn off the heat and stir in the sesame oil and scallions. Discard any unopened mussels.

7. Transfer to a serving dish and serve immediately.

Variation Tip

To boost the flavor profile, garnish with freshly chopped cilantro in place of the scallion.

KUNG PAO SHRIMP

FOR THE SAUCE

2 tablespoons rice vinegar

2 tablespoons soy sauce

2 teaspoons brown sugar

1 teaspoon dark soy sauce

1 teaspoon sesame oil

1 teaspoon cornstarch

FOR THE STIR-FRY

2 tablespoons peanut oil

8 to 10 dried red chiles

1 small green bell pepper
(or ½ a large one), cut
into bite-size pieces

2-inch piece ginger, peeled
and julienned

2 garlic cloves, minced

1 pound shrimp, peeled
and deveined

¼ cup unsalted
roasted peanuts

1 or 2 scallions, cut into
1-inch pieces

SERVES 4 TO 6 AS PART OF A MULTICOURSE MEAL /
PREP TIME: 5 MINUTES / COOK TIME: 10 MINUTES

This seafood spin on the Chinese-American classic features shrimp, bell pepper, and roasted peanuts covered in a savory and slightly (or very) spicy sauce. A feast for the senses, and it's ready in just 15 minutes.

1. In a small bowl, prepare the sauce by combining the rice vinegar, soy sauce, brown sugar, dark soy sauce, sesame oil, and cornstarch. Set it aside.

2. In a wok over medium heat, heat the peanut oil.

3. Add the chiles and bell pepper and stir-fry slowly, allowing the skin of the bell pepper to blister.

4. Add the ginger and garlic and stir fry for about 20 seconds until aromatic.

5. Add the shrimp, spreading them in a single layer. Cook the bottom side of the shrimp, then flip and stir-fry them for about 1 minute or until fully cooked.

6. Add the roasted peanuts and stir in the sauce.

7. When the sauce thickens, turn off the heat and toss in the scallions. Transfer to a serving dish and serve with steamed rice.

Cooking Tip

To make this dish extra spicy, halve or quarter the dried red chiles before tossing them in the wok. You can also add a sliced fresh red or green chile pepper when stir-frying the bell pepper.

HONEY-WALNUT SHRIMP

SERVES 4 TO 6 AS PART OF A MULTICOURSE MEAL /
PREP TIME: 5 MINUTES, PLUS 30 MINUTES FOR "CURING" /
COOK TIME: 5 MINUTES

FOR THE SHRIMP MARINADE

2 teaspoons baking soda
1 pound shrimp, peeled
    and deveined
Pinch salt
Pinch ground white pepper

FOR THE WALNUTS

¼ cup sugar
¼ cup water
½ cup walnuts

FOR THE SAUCE

1½ tablespoons mayonnaise
1 teaspoon honey
1 teaspoon sweetened
    condensed milk
½ teaspoon lemon juice

FOR THE STIR-FRY

2 tablespoons peanut oil
3 teaspoons cornstarch

Honey-walnut shrimp is one of my family's favorite dishes. This slightly healthier version features pan-fried instead of deep-fried shrimp, a light coating of sauce, and a generous serving of candied walnuts for added crunch.

1. Pour the baking soda over the shrimp and gently massage it into the shrimp. Let the shrimp rest in the refrigerator for 30 minutes, then thoroughly wash off the baking soda. Use a paper towel to blot any excess water from the shrimp. Sprinkle with the salt and pepper.

2. While the shrimp is marinating in the cornstarch, pour the sugar and water into a wok over medium-high heat. Stir until the syrup turns a light caramel color. Pour in the walnuts, stirring to coat. After about 1 minute, pour the walnuts onto parchment paper or aluminum foil and spread them out with a wok spatula. Let them cool.

3. In a small bowl, prepare the sauce by combining the mayonnaise, honey, condensed milk, and lemon juice. Set it aside.

4. In a wok over medium-high heat, heat the peanut oil.

5. Dredge the shrimp in the cornstarch, shake off the excess, and place them in the wok in a single layer. Cook for about 1 minute on one side, then stir-fry until they are fully cooked and transfer them to a bowl.

6. Add the candied walnuts to the shrimp, followed by the sauce, stirring to coat.

7. Serve immediately.

Cooking Tip

In case you were wondering why you marinate the shrimp in baking soda, this process gives the shrimp the bouncy, crunchy texture you experience at Chinese restaurants.

Variation Tip

For a crunchy snack with protein, indulge in the candied walnuts in this dish (just complete step 2).

Better Than Takeout

Each 3.7-ounce serving of Honey-Walnut Shrimp at Panda Express has 360 calories (of which 200 are from fat) and 35 grams of carbohydrates. With my recipe, the same serving size contains 233 calories (111 from fat) and 15 grams of carbs.

SHRIMP WITH LOBSTER SAUCE

FOR THE SAUCE

1 cup Basic Chinese Chicken
    Stock (page 25), or
    store bought
2 teaspoons soy sauce
2 teaspoons cornstarch
1 teaspoon Shaoxing wine
½ teaspoon sugar
Pinch ground white pepper

FOR THE STIR-FRY

1 tablespoon peanut oil
2-inch piece ginger, peeled
    and julienned
2 garlic cloves, minced
½ cup frozen peas and carrots
1 pound large shrimp, peeled
    and deveined
1 egg, lightly beaten

SERVES 4 TO 6 AS PART OF A MULTICOURSE MEAL /
PREP TIME: 5 MINUTES / COOK TIME: 5 MINUTES

I had not heard of shrimp with lobster sauce until I moved to the US. I was so confused the first time I ordered it—why was there no lobster in the sauce? Instead, the dish had large, succulent shrimp served in a thick gravy with egg, carrots, and green peas. Once you get past the surprise (no lobster), it's scrumptious.

1. In a small bowl, prepare the sauce by combining the chicken stock, soy sauce, cornstarch, Shaoxing wine, sugar, and pepper. Stir well, breaking up any lumps. Set it aside.

2. In a wok over medium-high heat, heat the peanut oil.

3. Add the ginger and garlic and stir-fry until aromatic, or for about 20 seconds.

4. Add the frozen peas and carrots and stir-fry for 10 seconds.

5. Pour in the sauce and the shrimp. Stir with a wok spatula to combine all the ingredients.

6. Slowly pour in the beaten egg while using the wok spatula to swirl it into the sauce.

7. As soon as the shrimp are cooked (they curl into a "C" shape), transfer the dish to a serving plate and serve immediately.

Serving Tip

Pair this dish with steamed white or brown rice (pages 20 and 22) to sop up all that good sauce.

Variation Tip

Some versions of this dish include ground pork. To use ground pork in the sauce, add about ¼ pound of ground pork to the wok after frying the ginger and garlic, and before adding the peas and carrots.

SPICY GARLIC SHRIMP

FOR THE SAUCE

1 tablespoon Basic Sambal
   (page 29)
1 tablespoon soy sauce
1 teaspoon Chinese
   black vinegar or apple
   cider vinegar
1 teaspoon brown sugar
½ teaspoon dark soy sauce

FOR THE STIR-FRY

2 tablespoons peanut oil
3 garlic cloves, minced
1 pound shrimp, peeled
   and deveined
1 scallion, chopped

SERVES 4 TO 6 AS PART OF A MULTICOURSE MEAL /
PREP TIME: 5 MINUTES / COOK TIME 5 MINUTES

This flavorful dish is perfect for even the busiest weeknight. I almost always have frozen shrimp on hand in the freezer and the sauce ingredients in the pantry. Even with the time it takes to thaw the shrimp under cold running water, it still cooks faster than the rice in the rice cooker—which of course pairs perfectly with it!

1. In a small bowl, prepare the sauce by combining the sambal, soy sauce, vinegar, brown sugar, and dark soy sauce. Set it aside.

2. In a wok over medium-high heat, heat the peanut oil.

3. Add the garlic and stir-fry until aromatic, or for about 20 seconds.

4. Add the shrimp and stir-fry until cooked, for 1 to 2 minutes.

5. When the shrimp is cooked through, add the sauce and stir to coat the shrimp.

6. Transfer the shrimp to a serving dish and garnish with the chopped scallion.

Variation Tips

To make this dish non-spicy, substitute ketchup for the sambal. Add cilantro along with the scallion garnish for a flavor twist.

SHRIMP AND BROCCOLI STIR-FRY

1 teaspoon Shaoxing wine
½ teaspoon salt
Pinch ground white pepper
2 teaspoons cornstarch
½ pound large shrimp,
    peeled and deveined

FOR THE SAUCE

2 tablespoons soy sauce
2 teaspoons oyster sauce
2 teaspoons rice vinegar
½ teaspoon sesame oil
½ teaspoon sugar

FOR THE STIR-FRY

1 tablespoon peanut oil
1-inch piece ginger, peeled
    and julienned
2 garlic cloves, minced
2 heads broccoli,
    cut into florets
1 carrot, peeled and sliced
1 teaspoon toasted
    sesame seeds
1 scallion, chopped

SERVES 6 TO 8 AS PART OF A MULTICOURSE MEAL /
PREP TIME: 5 MINUTES, PLUS 10 MINUTES TO MARINATE /
COOK TIME: 5 MINUTES

Here's a super-simple weeknight meal that's low in calories and tastes amazing. The crunchy broccoli and tender shrimp give this dish superb texture. It's great with or without rice, as the broccoli is quite filling.

1. In a medium bowl, pour the Shaoxing wine, salt, pepper and cornstarch over the shrimp, and toss to combine. Marinate at room temperature for 10 minutes.

2. Meanwhile, prepare the sauce by combining the soy sauce, oyster sauce, rice vinegar, sesame oil, and sugar.

3. In a wok over medium-high heat, heat the peanut oil.

4. Add the ginger and garlic, and stir-fry until aromatic, or for about 20 seconds. Add the broccoli florets and carrot, and stir-fry for about 1 minute.

5. Add the shrimp and the sauce to the wok. Stir-fry until the shrimp are cooked and the vegetables have softened.

6. Sprinkle the sesame seeds over the dish and stir to combine.

7. Transfer to a serving dish, garnish with the scallion, and serve immediately.

Cooking Tip

Feel free to adjust the crunchiness of the broccoli by adjusting its cooking time. If you like broccoli very soft, you may wish to steam it for about 5 minutes before adding it to the wok (or even ahead of time). Alternatively, you can thaw frozen broccoli, as it tends to be softer than fresh broccoli.

SALT AND PEPPER SHRIMP

3 tablespoons cornstarch

1 teaspoon freshly ground
black pepper

1 teaspoon sea salt

1 pound large shrimp,
deveined, tail on

2 tablespoons peanut oil

½ jalapeño or 1 Thai bird's eye
chile, thinly sliced (optional)

1 sprig fresh cilantro,
roughly chopped

SERVES 4 TO 6 AS PART OF A MULTICOURSE MEAL /
PREP TIME: 5 MINUTES / COOK TIME: 5 MINUTES

Salt and Pepper Shrimp is packed with flavor and spice.
Traditionally the shrimp are deep-fried, but here we pan-fry
them instead. You can make the dish extra spicy by adding
sliced jalapeño or even super spicy with finely sliced Thai
bird's eye chile. You can also cook the shrimp with the shells
on—the seared shells impart a special charred flavor.

1. In a medium bowl, combine the cornstarch, pepper,
and sea salt. Mix well and set it aside.

2. Just before frying the shrimp, add the shrimp to the
cornstarch mixture and toss to coat.

3. In a wok over medium-high heat, heat the peanut oil.

4. Shake any excess cornstarch off the shrimp and place
them in the wok in a single layer.

5. Allow the shrimp to cook on one side for about
30 seconds before flipping.

6. Add the sliced jalapeño or chile to the wok (if using)
and gently stir-fry to combine.

7. Transfer to a serving dish and garnish with the cilantro.

Ingredient Tip

Since salt is one of the starring ingredients in this dish,
experiment with different types of salt, such as Himalayan
salt and Celtic sea salt. They are considered the best and
healthiest salt varieties.

SEAFOOD CONGEE

1 cup short-grain rice

6 cups water, plus more
for rinsing rice

2-inch piece ginger, peeled,
plus 1-inch piece,
julienned, for garnish

2 teaspoons salt

1 (¾-pound) cod, tilapia, or
halibut fillet, cut into
bite-size pieces

6 to 8 large shrimp, each cut
into two or three pieces

½ cup bay scallops

2 teaspoons sesame oil

½ cup fresh cilantro leaves

1 scallion, chopped

SERVES 4 TO 6 / PREP TIME: 10 MINUTES / COOK TIME: 1 HOUR

Congee, warm and soothing, is often the comfort food I crave
when I'm feeling under the weather. The regular version can
be found on page 24, but here the fresh seafood adds incredible depth of flavor, making it even more luxurious.

1. Wash and rinse the uncooked rice under cold tap water
2 to 3 times. Drain as much of the water as possible. Alternatively, put the rice in a mesh strainer and rinse under
running tap water.

2. Place the rice, 6 cups of water, and peeled ginger in a
large pot.

3. Bring the water to a boil then reduce the heat to low.

4. Simmer, partially uncovered, for about 1 hour, stirring
occasionally to prevent sticking.

5. Increase the heat to medium and add the salt. Drop the
fish, shrimp, and scallops into the congee. Gently stir to
distribute the seafood evenly. Cook for 2 minutes, turn off
the heat, and stir in the sesame oil.

6. Serve warm with the cilantro leaves, chopped scallion,
and julienned ginger on the side.

Ingredient Tip

Traditionally, Chinese dried scallops are used in congee.
Although dried scallops provide a stronger taste, I prefer
the texture of fresh scallops for this recipe. You may wish to
experiment with both to see which type you prefer. If you
decide to use the large fresh diver scallops, I recommend cutting them into halves or quarters to ensure they cook quickly.

Dan Dan Noodles, page 163

Noodles & Rice

Cooking with Noodles and Rice

Rice and noodles are at the heart of Chinese cuisine. It is quite common, especially in southern China, to have rice with every meal (along with proteins and lots of vegetables, of course). Northern Chinese tend to prefer noodles. These noodles are usually stir-fried with proteins and vegetables or served in soup.

FRESH AND DRIED NOODLES

In China, noodles represent longevity. The longer, the better, and you should never, ever cut the noodles if they are being served at a birthday celebration! While there's a wide variety of noodles used in Chinese cooking, the two main types are egg noodles and rice noodles. Both can be found in different widths. Rice noodles can be as thin as a needle or more than an inch wide. The type of noodle you buy depends on the dish you are planning to cook. Read the recipe to find out the best noodle for that dish.

Dried noodles are convenient because they can keep for a year or two in your pantry. Cook them in boiling water for a few minutes, drain them, and serve them in a soup; or soak them in warm water to soften them if you are planning a stir-fry.

Fresh noodles can be found in the refrigerator or freezer section of Asian supermarkets. Most are stir-fry–ready, but always blanch them in boiling water for about a minute before serving them in soups.

THE DIFFERENCE BETWEEN LO MEIN AND CHOW MEIN

Even though lo mein and chow mein dishes may look the same and may even have the same ingredients, the cooking methods for the noodles are very different; that's what distinguishes them. *Lo mein* means stirred or tossed noodles, while *chow mein* means fried noodles.

To make lo mein, the accompanying ingredients such as meats and vegetables are stir-fried first. The heat is turned off, and the boiled noodles are added and stirred in the sauce just before serving.

Chow mein noodles can be made with varying degrees of crispiness, and even deep-fried. To make chow mein, the meats and vegetables are usually cooked, the noodles are fried over high heat, along with the sauce. Unlike lo mein, most fresh noodles do not have to be boiled ahead of time since they are fully cooked during stir-frying.

TYPES OF RICE

Medium- to long-grain white rice is normally used in Chinese cuisine because of the really nice texture and crunch it has if cooked correctly. My favorite type of white rice is jasmine rice, for its incredible fragrance. Short-grain rice is a little stickier and clumps together, so it's not ideal for steaming; however, the short-grain version is perfect for congee.

Whole-grain brown rice is healthier than white rice. It is essentially the same grain as white rice but with the bran layer and all the good nutritious stuff still intact. Brown rice has a different aroma and texture than white; it's got a bit of a nutty flavor and is chewier. Brown rice is a wonderful substitute for white rice in any dish, even in fried rice.

FRIED RICE TIPS

The best rice for fried rice is medium- or long-grain rice, because the grains separate easily. This is the best strategy for making perfect fried rice: Make a batch of steamed rice the day before you plan to make fried rice and let it sit in the refrigerator overnight. This gives the rice time to dry out a little, which preps it for stir-frying; the rice grains will separate nicely and get evenly seasoned.

To prepare cold rice for frying after sitting overnight in the refrigerator, wet your hands (to prevent sticking) and break up the clumps of rice with your fingers.

If you forgot to cook the rice the day before or if you suddenly need to have fried rice now, don't worry. Cook the rice as you normally would, but with about a cup less water. When the rice is cooked, fluff it up and then let it cool uncovered.

QUINOA FRIED RICE

2 tablespoons peanut oil

2 eggs, lightly beaten

3 garlic cloves, minced

3 or 4 string beans, cut into ¼-inch pieces

1 cup frozen peas and carrots (no need to thaw)

6 cups Steamed Quinoa (page 23)

2 tablespoons soy sauce

1 scallion, chopped

SERVES 4 TO 6 / PREP TIME: 10 MINUTES / COOK TIME: 5 MINUTES

For those of us who are trying to stay away from carbs but can't let go of fried rice, fried quinoa is a fantastic option. This ancient, grain-like seed from South America imparts everything you love about fried rice, and is packed with protein.

1. In a wok over medium-high heat, heat the peanut oil.

2. In the wok, scramble the eggs until cooked, then transfer them to a small bowl.

3. Add the garlic to the wok and stir-fry for about 20 seconds. Add the string beans and stir-fry for 20 to 30 seconds.

4. Add more peanut oil if necessary, then add the peas and carrots, and stir-fry for 30 seconds.

5. Add the quinoa and return the scrambled egg to the wok, stirring to combine.

6. Add the soy sauce. Stir-fry gently to combine, using a wok spatula.

7. Transfer to a serving dish and garnish with the chopped scallion.

Cooking Tip

Quinoa is much lighter than rice. Remember this when stir-frying—if you have a heavy hand, you could end up with quinoa all over your stove top!

Better Than Takeout

A typical 9.3-ounce serving of fried rice at Panda Express has 520 calories, 16 grams of fat, 120 grams of cholesterol, 850 grams of sodium, and 85 grams of carbs. By comparison, going healthy with this Quinoa Fried Rice recipe will give you 335 calories, 9 grams of fat, 74 milligrams of cholesterol, 186 milligrams of sodium, and 47 grams of carbs.

YANGZHOU FRIED RICE

2 tablespoons peanut oil (divided), plus more as needed

2 eggs, lightly beaten

½ pound shrimp, peeled and deveined

1 small onion, diced

½ cup diced ham

½ cup frozen peas (no need to thaw)

6 cups cooked white or brown rice (about 2 cups uncooked)

1 teaspoon salt

2 pinches ground white pepper

2 teaspoons soy sauce

3 scallions, finely chopped

SERVES 4 TO 6 / PREP TIME: 10 MINUTES / COOK TIME: 10 MINUTES

Of all the styles of fried rice, Yangzhou Fried Rice is a favorite in both Chinese households and restaurants. It's so popular that some restaurants call it House Fried Rice. It features shrimp, scrambled egg, diced ham or barbecue pork, and green peas.

1. In a wok over medium-high heat, heat 1 tablespoon of peanut oil.

2. Pour the eggs into the wok, cook until firm, and use a wok spatula to break the egg into small pieces. Remove the egg from the wok and set it aside.

3. Add a little more peanut oil to the wok if needed, add the shrimp, and stir-fry until fully cooked. Remove and set aside with the egg.

4. Add the remaining 1 tablespoon of oil to the wok, and swirl with the wok spatula to coat the bottom surface.

5. Add the onion and diced ham and stir-fry until the onion turns slightly translucent.

6. Add the frozen peas and stir-fry for a few seconds.

7. Add the cooked rice, sprinkle it with the salt and pepper, and drizzle with the soy sauce. Stir-fry for about 1 minute to season and heat the rice.

8. Return the scrambled egg and shrimp to the wok, and add the chopped scallions, stirring to combine all the ingredients.

9. Serve immediately.

Ingredient Tip

Cut the raw shrimp in half or thirds to get more shrimp in every bite!

SPICY SAMBAL FRIED RICE

3 tablespoons peanut oil
(divided)

2 eggs, lightly beaten

½ pound shrimp, peeled
and deveined

2 garlic cloves

¼ cup frozen diced carrots and
peas (no need to thaw)

2 tablespoons Basic Sambal
(page 29)

6 cups cooked white or brown
rice (about 2 cups uncooked)

½ teaspoon salt

¼ cup chopped fresh
cilantro leaves

SERVES 4 TO 6 / PREP TIME: 10 MINUTES /
COOK TIME: 10 MINUTES

Spicy sambal fried rice is inspired by Malaysian "Nyonya" cuisine. Nyonya refers to the cultural fusion born from the intermingling of ethnically Chinese and Malay people in Malaysia, a fusion evident in their cuisines. You can use the sambal recipe as indicated, or experiment with your favorite store-bought chili paste.

1. In a wok over high heat, heat 2 tablespoons of peanut oil.

2. Pour the eggs into the wok, cook until firm, and use a wok spatula to break the cooked egg into small pieces. Remove the egg from the wok and set it aside.

3. Add the shrimp to the wok. When the shrimp are about halfway cooked, add the garlic and stir-fry until the shrimp are fully cooked. Remove the shrimp and set them aside with the egg.

4. Add the remaining 1 tablespoon of oil to the wok. Add the diced carrots and peas, followed by the sambal. Stir-fry for about 30 seconds.

5. Add the cooked rice and salt, and stir-fry until the rice is evenly coated with the sambal.

6. Return the eggs and shrimp to the wok and stir to combine all the ingredients.

7. Garnish with the cilantro just before serving.

Substitution Tip

Feel free to swap out the cilantro for chopped scallion.

Variation Tip

Instead of scrambled egg, fry individual sunny-side up eggs for each serving and place them on top of the rice on individual plates. The runny yolk pairs perfectly with the spicy rice.

CHINESE SAUSAGE FRIED RICE

1 tablespoon peanut oil
1 Chinese sausage (lap cheong) link, sliced very thinly
1 carrot, diced
2 garlic cloves, minced
4 cups cooked white or brown rice (pages 20 and 22)
½ teaspoon salt
Pinch sugar
Pinch ground white pepper
2 scallions (green parts only), finely chopped

SERVES 4 / PREP TIME: 10 MINUTES / COOK TIME: 10 MINUTES

Chinese sausage, or *lap cheong*, is packed with so much sweet and savory flavor that you don't need much else to make a good fried rice. Since Chinese sausage contains quite a bit of marbling, it is cut into almost paper-thin slices to get the most taste into each bite and keep this dish as healthy as possible.

1. In a wok over medium-high heat, heat the peanut oil.

2. Add the sausage slices and stir-fry just until they start to brown. Remove and set them aside.

3. Add the carrot and stir-fry for about 1 minute. Add the garlic and stir-fry for about 20 seconds.

4. Add the rice, salt, sugar, and pepper. Return the Chinese sausage to the wok, then stir to combine the ingredients and turn off the heat.

5. Add the chopped scallions, stir to combine, and serve immediately.

Variation Tips

Try this dish with green peas instead of carrots, or use both. Add scrambled egg for a protein boost.

FRIED VERMICELLI NOODLES

1 (8-ounce) package dried
   rice vermicelli noodles
4 to 6 large dried shiitake
   mushrooms
Water for soaking noodles
   and mushrooms

FOR THE SAUCE

¼ cup soy sauce
2 tablespoons water
1 teaspoon dark soy sauce
½ teaspoon sugar
2 pinches ground white pepper

FOR THE STIR-FRY

2 tablespoons peanut oil
2 garlic cloves, minced
2 cups shredded cabbage
2 cups fresh mung bean
   sprouts, rinsed
2 scallions, cut into
   1-inch pieces

SERVES 4 / PREP TIME: 5 MINUTES, PLUS 30 MINUTES TO SOAK /
COOK TIME: 10 MINUTES

Rice vermicelli noodles are highly versatile; there are endless versions of this fried vermicelli recipe. You can add all sorts of proteins, vegetables, sauces, and seasonings. This is a super-simple version that we often prepare on lazy Sunday mornings.

1. In a large bowl, soak the noodles in warm water. In a small bowl, soak the shiitake mushrooms in hot water. Allow about 30 minutes for the noodles and the mushrooms to soften.

2. Drain the noodles in a colander, and set them aside.

3. Cut the mushrooms into thin strips.

4. In a small bowl, prepare the sauce by mixing together the soy sauce, water, dark soy sauce, sugar, and pepper. Set it aside.

5. In a wok over medium-high heat, heat the peanut oil.

6. Add the garlic and stir-fry until aromatic, for about 20 seconds.

7. Toss in the cabbage and stir-fry until slightly wilted.

8. Add the vermicelli noodles and the sauce. Stir-fry for about 5 minutes, until the noodles have absorbed all the liquid.

9. Add the bean sprouts and scallions, and stir-fry just to mix them into the noodles.

10. Transfer to a serving plate and serve immediately.

Variation Tips

Add chicken, pork, or tofu for protein, or replace cabbage with shredded bok choy, choy sum, or leafy greens.

SHRIMP HOR FUN
(FLAT RICE NOODLES IN GRAVY)

FOR THE GRAVY

2 cups Basic Chinese Chicken
   Stock (page 25), or
   store bought
½ cup water
3 tablespoons cornstarch
2 tablespoons soy sauce
2 teaspoons oyster sauce
1 teaspoon Shaoxing wine
½ teaspoon sugar
2 pinches ground white pepper

FOR THE STIR-FRY

2 tablespoons peanut oil,
   plus 2 teaspoons
1 pound fresh flat rice noodles
1½ tablespoons soy
   sauce, divided
¾ teaspoon dark soy
   sauce, divided
½ pound rice vermicelli
   noodles, soaked in warm
   water for 30 minutes
2 garlic cloves, minced
10 to 12 large shrimp,
   peeled and deveined
1 stalk choy sum or 2 baby bok
   choy, cut into 1-inch pieces
1 small carrot, sliced

SERVES 4 TO 6 / PREP TIME: 10 MINUTES /
COOK TIME: 10 MINUTES

This dish, also known as seafood chow fun, features two kinds of fried rice noodles in a thick seafood gravy. The vermicelli noodles mix with the flat noodles for a unique texture.

1. In a large bowl, prepare the gravy by mixing the chicken stock, water, cornstarch, soy sauce, oyster sauce, Shaoxing wine, sugar, and pepper. Set it aside.

2. In a wok over high heat, heat 2 tablespoons of peanut oil.

3. Add the flat rice noodles and stir in 1 tablespoon of soy sauce and ½ teaspoon of dark soy sauce. Stir-fry slowly for about 1 minute, being careful not to over-stir so as to allow some parts of the noodles to get slightly charred. Remove the flat noodles from the wok and set them aside.

4. Add the vermicelli noodles, the remaining ½ tablespoon of soy sauce, and the remaining ¼ teaspoon of dark soy sauce. Stir-fry for about 1 minute.

5. Return the flat rice noodles to the wok, stirring just to combine with the vermicelli noodles. Remove from the wok and set aside.

6. Reduce the heat to medium-high and add the remaining 2 teaspoons of oil to the wok.

7. Add the garlic and stir-fry for about 20 seconds, until aromatic.

8. Pour the gravy into the wok. Add the shrimp, choy sum, and carrot. Gently stir and allow the gravy to boil for about 1 minute. Transfer to a large bowl.

9. When ready to serve, pour the gravy, shrimp, and vegetable mixture over the fried noodles.

Ingredient Tip

If you can't find fresh flat rice noodles, you can use dried flat rice noodles. Buy the largest or widest noodles you can find. Cooking time will depend on the size of the noodles. Add the dried noodles to boiling water and cook until al dente.

BEEF CHOW FUN

FOR THE BEEF MARINADE

1 teaspoon soy sauce
1 teaspoon oyster sauce
Pinch freshly ground
    black pepper
2 teaspoons cornstarch
½ pound sirloin steak
    or tenderloin, cut into
    thin strips

FOR THE SAUCE

2 tablespoons soy sauce
2 teaspoons dark soy sauce
2 teaspoons Shaoxing wine
½ teaspoon brown sugar
Pinch ground white pepper

FOR THE STIR-FRY

1 pound fresh flat rice noodles
    (or about 8 ounces dried flat
    noodles, soaked in warm
    water until al dente)
2 tablespoons peanut oil,
    divided, plus more if needed
2 garlic cloves, minced
½ small onion, cut into
    thin slices
2 cups fresh bean
    sprouts, rinsed
2 scallions, cut into
    1-inch pieces

SERVES 4 TO 6 / PREP TIME: 5 MINUTES, PLUS 15 MINUTES TO MARINATE / COOK TIME: 5 MINUTES

This favorite Cantonese noodle dish combines stir-fried flat rice noodles with crisp fresh bean sprouts and slices of beef with sweet and salty seasoning. The noodles are fried quickly in a very hot wok over high heat, giving the dish that *wok hei* ("breath of the wok") essence.

1. Pour the soy sauce, oyster sauce, pepper, and cornstarch over the beef, and toss to coat. Marinate at room temperature for 15 minutes.

2. Gently separate the flat rice noodles so they are not clumpy. Drizzle some peanut oil over the noodles to loosen them if necessary.

3. In a small bowl, prepare the sauce by mixing together the soy sauce, dark soy sauce, Shaoxing wine, brown sugar, and white pepper. Set it aside.

4. In a wok over medium-high heat, heat 1 tablespoon of peanut oil. Add the beef and stir-fry just until no longer pink. Remove it and set it aside.

5. Add the remaining 1 tablespoon of oil to the wok, then toss in the garlic and onion. Stir-fry just until the onion becomes translucent.

6. Increase the heat to high. Add the flat rice noodles to the wok, separating them, then add the sauce. Stir-fry until all the noodles are evenly coated.

7. Return the beef to the wok. Toss in the bean sprouts and scallions at the last minute and turn off the heat.

8. Serve immediately.

Variation Tips

Fried chow fun can be spun many ways. Instead of beef, try chicken, pork, or shrimp, or even a combination of several proteins. For a healthy spin, add Chinese vegetables like bok choy or kai lan.

CHICKEN CHOW MEIN

FOR THE CHICKEN MARINADE

2 teaspoons soy sauce

1 teaspoon oyster sauce

2 teaspoons cornstarch

1 (5-ounce) chicken breast,
   cut into bite-size pieces

FOR THE SAUCE

2 tablespoons soy sauce

1 tablespoon oyster sauce

2 teaspoons Shaoxing wine

1 teaspoon brown sugar

1 teaspoon sesame oil

½ teaspoon salt

2 pinches ground white pepper

FOR THE STIR-FRY

2 tablespoons peanut oil,
   plus more if needed

2 garlic cloves, minced

2 cups shredded cabbage

1 small carrot, julienned

1 pound fresh chow mein
   noodles or fresh egg
   noodles, cooked according
   to package directions

2 scallions, cut into
   1-inch pieces

SERVES 4 TO 6 / PREP TIME: 10 MINUTES, PLUS 20 MINUTES
TO MARINATE / COOK TIME: 5 MINUTES

Chow mein is arguably the most popular noodle dish in
Chinese-American cuisine. Some Chinese restaurants will
even allow you to swap your rice for chow mein—just ask!
This healthier homemade version includes lots of protein
and vegetables.

1. Pour the soy sauce, oyster sauce, and cornstarch over the
chicken in a medium bowl and marinate at room temperature
for 20 minutes.

2. In a small bowl, prepare the sauce by combining the soy
sauce, oyster sauce, Shaoxing wine, brown sugar, sesame
oil, salt, and pepper.

3. In a wok over medium-high heat, heat the peanut oil. As
soon as the wok starts to smoke, add the chicken and stir-fry
until fully cooked. Remove the chicken and set it aside.

4. Add a little more oil to the wok if needed, add the garlic, and stir-fry for about 20 seconds, until aromatic.

5. Add the shredded cabbage and carrot, and stir-fry until the cabbage wilts slightly.

6. Add the noodles, stir in the sauce, and return the chicken to the wok.

7. Stir-fry for about 1 minute, combining all the ingredients.

8. Turn off the heat, add the scallions, and stir to combine. Transfer to a serving dish.

Ingredient Tip

If the fresh noodles are a bit sticky, toss them in a bit of peanut oil or olive oil. This will help separate them and also prevent them from sticking to the wok.

VEGETABLE LO MEIN

8 ounces lo mein or
  egg noodles
Water for boiling noodles

FOR THE SAUCE

2 tablespoons soy sauce
1 tablespoon dark soy sauce
2 teaspoons oyster sauce
1 teaspoon brown sugar
1 teaspoon sesame oil

FOR THE STIR-FRY

2 tablespoons peanut oil
2-inch piece ginger, peeled
  and julienned
2 garlic cloves, minced
6 large whole dried shiitake
  mushrooms, soaked and
  cut into thin strips
4 ounces fresh snow peas
1 small carrot, julienned
2 stalks baby bok choy,
  cut into ½-inch strips

SERVES 4 / PREP TIME: 10 MINUTES / COOK TIME: 5 MINUTES

The range of vegetables you can use in this lo mein recipe is endless; mix it up with sliced bell pepper, baby spinach, baby corn, broccolini, sugar snap peas, or green peas. Simply stir-fry the vegetables, turn off the heat, add the noodles, and stir in the sauce. Voilà, dinner is served!

1. If using fresh noodles, boil them for about 30 seconds and drain. If using dried noodles, boil them until al dente and drain.

2. In a small bowl, prepare the sauce by combining the soy sauce, dark soy sauce, oyster sauce, brown sugar, and sesame oil. Set it aside.

3. In a wok over medium-high heat, heat the peanut oil.

4. Add the ginger and garlic, and stir-fry until aromatic, or for about 20 seconds.

5. Add the mushrooms and snow peas. As soon as the snow peas turn bright green, toss in the carrot and bok choy. Stir-fry until the bok choy leaves have wilted.

6. Turn off the heat and add the noodles and sauce. Stir just to combine.

7. Transfer to a serving dish and serve immediately.

Substitution Tip

If you are not able to find lo mein noodles, you can use whole-wheat thin spaghetti or ramen instead. Prepare according to the package directions.

DAN DAN NOODLES

1 pound fresh Chinese egg noodles (or about 8 ounces dried noodles), cooked according to package instructions

2 teaspoons peanut oil

½-inch piece ginger, peeled and julienned

2 garlic cloves, minced

½ pound ground pork

2 teaspoons soy sauce

1 teaspoon dark soy sauce

½ teaspoon brown sugar

½ teaspoon salt

Pinch ground white pepper

1 tablespoon peanut oil

1 teaspoon ground Sichuan peppercorns

2 garlic cloves, minced

½ cup Basic Chinese Chicken Stock (page 25), or store bought

2 teaspoons rice vinegar

2 teaspoons soy sauce

Pinch salt

Pinch ground white pepper

1 scallion, chopped

¼ cup unsalted roasted peanuts, chopped

SERVES 4 TO 6 / PREP TIME: 15 MINUTES / COOK TIME: 15 MINUTES

There are many versions of dan dan noodles, but typically, this Sichuan street food consists of fresh white noodles in a spicy broth topped with savory ground pork and ground peanuts. Like most Sichuan dishes, it can be very spicy, so feel free to reduce the amount of Sichuan peppercorns you use.

1. Rinse the prepared noodles under cold tap water, make sure most of the water is drained, and divide them evenly between serving bowls.

2. In a wok over medium heat, heat the peanut oil. Add the ginger and garlic and stir-fry until aromatic, about 20 seconds.

3. Add the ground pork and stir-fry until fully cooked. Add the soy sauce, dark soy sauce, brown sugar, salt, and pepper, mixing to combine. Distribute this pork mixture evenly among the serving bowls over the noodles.

4. Add the peanut oil, Sichuan peppercorns, and garlic to the wok, and stir-fry for about 20 seconds.

5. Into the wok, pour the chicken stock, rice vinegar, soy sauce, salt, and pepper, then stir to combine. Remove from the heat and divide the broth evenly over the pork in each serving bowl.

6. Garnish each bowl with the chopped scallion and peanuts.

Substitution Tips

If you can't find Sichuan peppercorns, substitute red pepper flakes. And instead of ground pork, try this dish with ground chicken or ground beef.

Resources

ASIAN MARKETS: Your local Asian markets and supermarkets are a fantastic resource, and shopping local is always the best option. Most of the time, you can just tell the grocers what recipe you're making (or show them a picture), and they'll tell you exactly what you need. They can even recommend popular brands of products that most restaurants use.

AMAZON.COM: An e-commerce platform where you'll be able to find most pantry and kitchen items needed for cooking any cuisine, including Asian. Some sellers even carry fresh items such as lemongrass and curry leaves. Amazon has a great selection of products from different brands and is often my go-to for hard-to-find items.

ASIANFOODGROCER.COM: Another e-commerce site, here you'll find a good variety of Asian products including snacks and sauces, housewares, kitchen utensils, and even adorable stationery. They carry mostly Japanese items but there are Chinese products as well.

EFOODDEPOT.COM: On this website, items are sorted by their country of origin, so it's easy to determine which products are authentic. You can also sort by brand, a convenient tool for finding exactly what you need from your trusted brands. They carry a good selection at reasonable prices.

WOKANDSKILLET.COM: This website is my online collection of simple Chinese and Asian-inspired recipes. Most recipes have step-by-step instructions and vibrant pictures.

WOKSHOP.COM: This website (with a brick-and-mortar location in San Francisco) contains an impressive selection of Chinese kitchenware, cooking tools, and woks, including carbon steel and the traditional cast iron. You'll also find all the accessories you need for wok cooking.

WORLDMARKET.COM: World Market has retail locations all over the United States, but you can also purchase items from its online store. It carries a decent selection of basic Chinese sauces, condiments, and pantry items. Nice kitchen utensils and dinnerware, too!

RECOMMENDED BRANDS:

CHICKEN STOCK GRANULES: Knorr (Chicken Seasoning Powder)

SOY SAUCE: Pearl River Bridge, Lee Kum Kee

HOISIN SAUCE: Lee Kum Kee

OYSTER SAUCE: Lee Kum Kee Premium Oyster Sauce

SESAME OIL: Kadoya Pure Sesame Oil

SHAOXING WINE: Shaohsing Rice Cooking Wine

Measurement Conversions

Volume Equivalents (Liquid)

US STANDARD	US STANDARD (OUNCES)	METRIC (APPROXIMATE)
2 tablespoons	1 fl. oz.	30 mL
¼ cup	2 fl. oz.	60 mL
½ cup	4 fl. oz.	120 mL
1 cup	8 fl. oz.	240 mL
1½ cups	12 fl. oz.	355 mL
2 cups or 1 pint	16 fl. oz.	475 mL
4 cups or 1 quart	32 fl. oz.	1 L
1 gallon	128 fl. oz.	4 L

Oven Temperatures

FAHRENHEIT (F)	CELSIUS (C) (APPROXIMATE)
250°	120°
300°	150°
325°	165°
350°	180°
375°	190°
400°	200°
425°	220°
450°	230°

Volume Equivalents (Dry)

US STANDARD	METRIC (APPROXIMATE)
⅛ teaspoon	0.5 mL
¼ teaspoon	1 mL
½ teaspoon	2 mL
¾ teaspoon	4 mL
1 teaspoon	5 mL
1 tablespoon	15 mL
¼ cup	59 mL
⅓ cup	79 mL
½ cup	118 mL
⅔ cup	156 mL
¾ cup	177 mL
1 cup	235 mL
2 cups or 1 pint	475 mL
3 cups	700 mL
4 cups or 1 quart	1 L

Weight Equivalents

US STANDARD	METRIC (APPROXIMATE)
½ ounce	15 g
1 ounce	30 g
2 ounces	60 g
4 ounces	115 g
8 ounces	225 g
12 ounces	340 g
16 ounces or 1 pound	455 g

Recipe Index

Index

Acknowledgements

This cookbook would not be possible without the support and encouragement of my family and friends.

First and foremost, thank you Mum, for being by my side throughout this entire process; not only with the cookbook but through every chapter of my life, no matter how difficult or challenging. I thank you for teaching me how to cook, and thank you for being such a great role model that I am so proud to look up to.

Thank you Dad, for your constant support and guidance. You taught me to chase my dreams and never give up; that anything is possible. Thank you for teaching me the meaning of selfless love.

To my best friend and husband, David: Thank you for always being there for me. Thank you for believing in me, for dreaming with me, and for loving me for who I am. I love you more and more every day.

To my sons, Jayden and Brennan: Thank you for making me smile. You make my heart so happy and I am so proud of you both.

To Tzen: Your love for food and great appetite encourages me to keep cooking and trying new recipes! Thank you for encouraging me and for being willing to try all of my recipes!

Special thanks to Linda Ooi for writing the foreword to this book. You are such an inspiration to me.

A big thank you to my taste-testers for this project: Amy Nash (Houseofnasheats.com), Bethany Arnold, Christi Cameron, Christine Leong & David Knight (Vermilionroots.com), Dawne Frain, Dhyana Wallace, Diane Cowell, Donna Mansour (Wholefoodbellies.com), Edwina Augustin, Felicitas Teoh (Gingerandcilantro.com), Jenni Ward (Thegingeredwhisk .com), Jessica Freimann (Thelifejolie.com), Kathy McDaniel (Lemonblossoms.com), Kylee Ayotte (Kyleecooks.com), Laura Mooney, Michele Hall (Westviamidwest.com), Mira Crisp (Foodsmartmom.com), Neli Howard (Deliciousmeetshealthy.com), Peter and Julia Foerster (Platedcravings.com), Shann & Jesse Ormsbee, Shelley Blechar (Chefintheburbs.com) and Sherene Cheah Milizia. Your feedback and advice were invaluable, and contributed to the creation of this book.

Writing a cookbook had been on my mind under my "someday" goals for a while, but I never dreamed that it would happen so quickly. A big thank you to Meg Ilasco and the team at Callisto Media for giving me this tremendous opportunity.

Thank you all from the bottom of my heart. I am forever grateful.

9 781623 158989